HOUGHTON MIFFLIN

MATHEMATICS

Skill Workbook

Grade 5

Houghton Mifflin Company • BOSTON

Atlanta • Dallas • Geneva, Illinois • Palo Alto • Princeton

This Skill Workbook contains all of the Skill Worksheets
from *Houghton Mifflin Mathematics Math Masters* in an
easy-to-manage workbook format.

Printed in U.S.A.
ISBN: 0-395-68011-5

123456789-BBS-98 97 96 95 94

Skill Workbook

Worksheet-to-Lesson Correlation

Module 1

Lesson	Skill Worksheet
1	1, 2, 3, 4
2	5, 6, 7, 8
3	9, 10, 11, 12
4	13, 14, 15, 16
5	17, 18
6	19, 20
7	21, 22, 23, 24
8	25, 26
9	27, 28, 29, 30, 31, 32

Module 2

Lesson	Skill Worksheet
1	33, 34, 35, 36
2	37, 38, 39, 40
3	41, 42
4	43, 44, 45, 46
5	47, 48
6	49, 50, 51, 52
7	53, 54, 55, 56
8	57, 58, 59, 60
9	61, 62, 63, 64

Skill Workbook

Worksheet-to-Lesson Correlation

Skill Workbook

Worksheet-to-Lesson Correlation

Module 5

Lesson	Skill Worksheet
1	129, 130, 131, 132
2	133, 134, 135, 136
3	137, 138, 139, 140
4	141, 142, 143, 144
5	145, 146, 147, 148
6	149, 150, 151, 152
7	153, 154, 155, 156
8	157, 158, 159, 160

Module 6

Lesson	Skill Worksheet
1	161, 162
2	163, 164
3	165, 166, 167, 168
4	169, 170, 171, 172
5	173, 174, 175, 176
6	177, 178, 179, 180
7	181, 182, 183, 184
8	185, 186, 187, 188
9	189, 190
10	191, 192

Skill Workbook

Worksheet-to-Lesson Correlation

Module 7

Lesson	Skill Worksheet
1	193, 194, 195, 196
2	197, 198, 199, 200
3	201, 202, 203, 204
4	205, 206, 207, 208
5	209, 210, 211, 212
6	213, 214, 215, 216
7	217, 218, 219, 220
8	221, 222, 223, 224

Module 8

Lesson	Skill Worksheet
1	225, 226, 227, 228
2	229, 230, 231, 232
3	233, 234, 235, 236
4	237, 238, 239, 240
5	241, 242
6	243, 244
7	245, 246, 247, 248
8	249, 250, 251, 252
9	253, 254, 255, 256

Name _____

Is the pattern a polyomino?

1.

2.

_____   _____

3.

4.

_____   _____

Add one square to make each figure a polyomino.

5.

6.

Module 1: Section A, Lesson 1

Name _____

Add squares to make four different polyominos that have six squares each.

1.

2.

3.

4.

Is each pair of polyominos congruent? For each congruent pair, write whether the second polyomino is a slide, flip, or turn of the first.

5.

6.

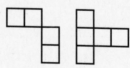

7.

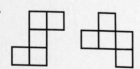

8.

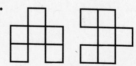

Module 1: Section A, Lesson 1

Name _____

For each congruent pair, write whether the second figure is a slide, flip, or turn of the first figure.

1.

_____

2.

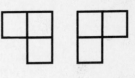

_____

3.

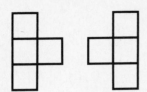

_____

4.

_____

5.

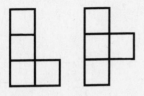

_____

6.

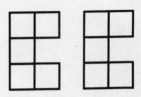

_____

Module 1: Section A, Lesson 1

Name _____

Draw a slide, a flip, and a turn of each figure below.

1.

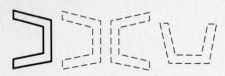

2.

3.

4.

3

5.

Module 1: Section A, Lesson 1

Name _____

Find the area and perimeter.

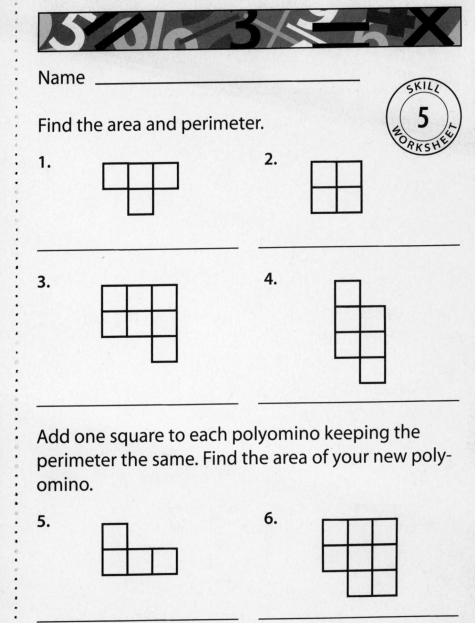

1.

2.

_____   _____

3.

4.

_____   _____

Add one square to each polyomino keeping the perimeter the same. Find the area of your new polyomino.

5.

6.

_____   _____

Module 1: Section A, Lesson 2

Name _____

For Figures 1 and 2, sketch a polyomino with the same perimeter. Find its area.

1.

2.

$A =$ _____ $A =$ _____

For Figures 3–6, sketch a polyomino with the same area and perimeter.

3.

4.

5.

6.

Module 1: Section A, Lesson 2

Name _____

Is each polyomino symmetrical? Answer *yes* or *no*.

1.

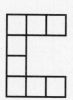

_____

2.

_____

3.

_____

4.

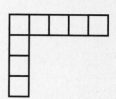

_____

5.

_____

6.

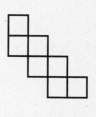

_____

Module 1: Section A, Lesson 2

Name _____

Draw a line of symmetry through each figure.

1.

2.

3.

4.

5.

6.

Sketch the following.

7. A five-square symmetrical polyomino with all lines of symmetry shown.

8. A five-square polyomino that is not symmetrical.

Module 1: Section A, Lesson 2

Name _____

SKILL
WORKSHEET
9

Sketch the following.

1. The first 4 steps of L-numbers.

2. Steps 4 to 6 of L-numbers.

3 The first 3 steps of square numbers.

4. Steps 3 to 5 of square numbers.

Multiply.

5. $8 \times 2 =$ _____

6. $7 \times 5 =$ _____

7. $3 \times 9 =$ _____

8. $6 \times 3 =$ _____

Name _____

How many counters are in the
L-number at each step?

1. 10th step

2. 15th step

_____   _____

3. 21st step

4. 24th step

_____   _____

How many counters are in the square number at
each step?

5. 10th step

6. 15th step

_____   _____

7. 21st step

8. 24th step

_____   _____

Multiply.

9. $4 \times 8 =$ _____   **10.** $7 \times 7 =$ _____

11. $5 \times 9 =$ _____   **12.** $6 \times 8 =$ _____

Module 1: Section B, Lesson 3

Name _____

1. Draw four steps of a growth pattern.

Step 1   Step 2

Step 3   Step 4

2. Record the number of counters in each step of your pattern.

_____

_____

3. Write a short description of your pattern.

_____

_____

Module 1: Section B, Lesson 3

Name _____

1. Here are the first two steps of a
growth pattern. Show two
possibilities for Step 3.

Step 1    Step 2

Step 3

Write two possibilities for Step 3 in the following
number patterns.

2. 4, 8, _____   **3.** 2, 6, _____

    4, 8, _____   2, 6, _____

4. 1, 4, _____   **5.** 6, 18, _____

    1, 4, _____   6, 18, _____

Module 1: Section B, Lesson 3

Name _____

Find the 10th number in each sequence. For each sequence, write the expression you used.

1. 7, 14, 21 _____ n _____

2. 1, 2, 3 _____ n _____

3. 4, 8, 12 _____ n _____

4. 9, 18, 27 _____ n _____

Find the 13th number in each sequence. Write the expression you used.

5. 5, 10, 15 _____ n _____

6. 8, 9, 10 _____ n _____

7. 13, 14, 15 _____ n _____

8. 6, 12, 18 _____ n _____

    Module 1: Section B, Lesson 4

Name _____

Find the 25th step in each sequence.
Use your calculator.

1. 9, 18, 27 _____   2. 10, 20, 30 _____

3. 20, 40, 60 _____ 4. 100, 200, 300 _____

Find the 100th step in each sequence in problems
1–4. Use your calculator.

5. _____   6. _____

7. _____   8. _____

For the four sequences in problems 1–4, write the
expression you used.

9. _____   10. _____

11. _____ 12. _____

13. Use a variable to write
your own expression. _____

14. Write the first 5 numbers
in your sequence. _____

Module 1: Section B, Lesson 4

Name _____

You receive an allowance of $3.00 per week. Imagine that you are able to save $.25 per week.

1. How much money will you save after 4 weeks? _____

2. How much money will you save after 42 days? _____

3. What expression did you use to get your answers? _____

You are planning a party. Each guest will get 3 prizes.

4. How many prizes will you need for 10 guests? _____

5. How many prizes will you need for 23 guests? _____

6. What expression did you use to get your answers? _____

Module 1: Section B, Lesson 4

Name _____

Your new puppy weighed 2 pounds when it was born. The puppy will gain 2 pounds per month for the first year.

1. What will the puppy weigh in two months? _____

2. What will the puppy weigh in eight months? _____

3. What expression did you use to get your answer? _____

Your friend rides 3 miles a week on her bicycle.

4. How many miles does your friend ride in 5 weeks? _____

5. How many miles does your friend ride in 28 days? _____

6. What expression did you use to get your answer? _____

Name _____

Materials: 2 copies of a hundred chart (Activity Worksheet 1)

Make a repeating two-color pattern on a hundred chart.

1. What patterns do you see in the chart? _____

2. Why are the columns the same color in this chart? _____

3. Why do the diagonals alternate color in this chart? _____

Make a repeating six-color pattern on another hundred chart.

4. What patterns do you see in the six-color chart? _____

5. On which chart do the numbers 5 and 65 share the same color? _____

6. On which chart do the numbers 8 and 38 share the same color? _____

Module 1: Section C, Lesson 5

Name _____

Think about patterns on a hundred chart.

1. Do the numbers 2 and 18 share the same color on a two-color pattern? _____

   on a four-color pattern? _____

2. Do the numbers 16 and 64 share the same color on a four-color pattern? _____

   on a six-color pattern? _____

3. For a field trip, your class forms a line. The first student is put in group 1, the second in group 2, the third in group 3, the fourth in group 4, the fifth in group 5, the sixth in group 1, the seventh in group 2 and so on. If you want to be in the same group as your friend, who is fourth in line, where should you stand? _____

Write = or ≠ in the circle. Explain how you know.

4. $34 + 88 - 9$ ◯ $(34 + 88) - 9$ _____

5. $(94 - 56) - 8$ ◯ $94 - (56 + 8)$ _____

Module 1: Section C, Lesson 5

Name _____

Materials: hundred chart (Activity Worksheet 1)

Make a repeating seven-color pattern on a hundred chart.

1. Will the pattern show any stripes or diagonals?

_____

What color is each of the following squares?

2. 9 _____   **3.** 21 _____   **4.** 41 _____

5. 60 _____   **6.** 55 _____   **7.** 34 _____

8. 76 _____   **9.** 93 _____   **10.** 82 _____

If 1 is blue, 2 is white , 3 is yellow, and 4 is red in a repeating four-color pattern, what color is each of the following squares?

11. 41 _____   **12.** 19 _____   **13.** 77 _____

14. 52 _____   **15.** 95 _____   **16.** 89 _____

Module 1: Section C, Lesson 6

Name _____

Materials: hundred chart (Activity Worksheet 1)

In a repeating four-color pattern on a hundred chart, square 1 is blue, 2 is green, 3 is white, and 4 is yellow.

1. What color is square 55? _____

2. What color is square 17? _____

3. What are the next three squares after 69 that share the same color as square 6? _____

4. Will the squares 42 and 77 share the same color? _____ If they do not, what square closest to 77 will share the same color as 42? _____

5. What are the next three squares after 30 that share the same color as 56? _____

In a six-color repeating pattern, square 8 is blue, 37 is yellow, 59 is green, and 90 is white.

6. What color is square 1? _____

7. What color is square 6? _____

Name _____

Materials: hundred chart (Activity Worksheet 1)

1. Write an expression to go from 25 to 100 on the chart. _____

2. Write an expression to go from 12 to 57 on the chart. _____

3. Write a different expression to go from 12 to 57 on the chart. _____

4. Write an expression to go from 75 to 39 on the chart. _____

5. Write an expression to go from 53 to 5 on the chart. _____

Does each expression get you to 91 on the chart?

6. 4 + 70 + 20 _____   **7.** 28 – 20 + 80 + 3 _____

8. 54 + 30 – 3 _____   **9.** 61 – 30 + 1 + 60 – 1 _____

10. Write a different expression to get to 91 on the chart. _____

Module 1: Section C, Lesson 7

Name _____

Materials: hundred chart (Activity Worksheet 1)

1. Write an expression using *y*. Describe a move one space down diagonally
   right on the chart. _____

2. Write an expression using *y*. Describe a move four spaces down diagonally
   right on the chart. _____

3. Write an expression using *y*. Describe a move one space down diagonally
   left on the chart. _____

4. Write an expression using *y*. Describe a move five spaces down diagonally
   left on the chart. _____

5. Write an expression using *y*. Describe a move three spaces up diagonally
   left on the chart. _____

Module 1: Section C, Lesson 7

Name _____

Materials: hundred chart (Activity Worksheet 1)

Write two expressions that describe two different paths between each pair of numbers on the chart.

1. 28 to 56 _____

2. 32 to 70 _____

3. 15 to 62 _____

4. 2 to 18 _____

5. 78 to 91 _____

Find each value of *n* on the chart.

6. $n + 30 = 72$ _____

7. $50 - n = 32$ _____

8. $22 + n = 27$ _____

9. $99 - n = 44$ _____

10. $66 - n = 26$ _____

11. $55 + n = 66$ _____

12. $n + 18 = 39$ _____

13. $n + 11 = 14$ _____

14. $n + 26 = 38$ _____

15. $88 + n = 88$ _____

Module 1: Section C, Lesson 7

Name _____

Materials: hundred chart (Activity
Worksheet 1)

1. A path on a hundred chart starts at a square and
   goes three squares down, five right, and three up to
   30. Call the first square y and write an equation for
   this path. Find the value of y.

   _____

2. A path on the chart starts at a square and goes
   four squares up, nine left, and three down to 71.
   Call the first square y and write an equation for
   this path. Find the value of y.

   _____

Find the value of z on the chart.

3. $z - 20 = 58$ _____   4. $z - 11 = 71$ _____

5. $24 - z = 13$ _____   6. $38 - z = 31$ _____

7. $108 - z + 20 = 51$ _____ 8. $57 + z - 5 = 102$ _____

Module 1: Section C, Lesson 7

Name _____

Find the first five multiples of the
following numbers.

1. 4 _____   2. 7 _____

3. 9 _____   4. 8 _____

Write the first two common multiples of each pair of
numbers.

5. 2 and 4 _____   6. 3 and 4 _____

7. 4 and 12 _____   8. 5 and 11 _____

9. 2 and 6 _____   10. 3 and 6 _____

11. Which pairs of numbers in Exercises 5–10 have a
    common multiple that is the same as one of the
    numbers?

    _____

12. Which pairs of numbers in Exercises 5–10 have a
    least common multiple that is the product of the
    two numbers?

    _____

Module 1: Section D, Lesson 8

Name _____

Write the first two common multiples of each pair of numbers.

1. 3 and 5 _____

2. 8 and 9 _____

3. 2 and 10 _____

4. 1 and 8 _____

5. 6 and 7 _____

6. 11 and 12 _____

7. 5 and 9 _____

8. 3 and 7 _____

9. What pair of numbers has 27 as a common multiple? _____

10. What pair of numbers has 63 as a common multiple? _____

11. What is the least common multiple of 9 and 10? _____

12. What is the least common multiple of 10 and 12? _____

13. How do you know when the least common multiple is the product of a pair of numbers?

_____

Module 1: Section D, Lesson 8

Name _____

Find the factors of each number. Write
all the multiplication equations that
have each number as the product.

1. 16 _____

2. 12 _____

3. 9 _____

4. 36 _____

5. 48 _____

6. 43 _____

7. 80 _____

8. 100 _____

9. 25 _____

10. 95 _____

11. 49 _____

12. 61 _____

Module 1: Section D, Lesson 8

Name _____

1. Which numbers between 1 and 20 are divisible by 4?

_____

2. Which numbers between 1 and 50 are divisible by 8? _____

3. Which numbers between 50 and 80 are divisible by 6? _____

Is each number divisible by 5?

4. 81 _____   **5.** 65 _____   **6.** 35 _____

Is each number divisible by 9?

7. 89 _____   **8.** 56 _____   **9.** 81 _____

10. How many numbers between 1 and 10 do not have factors other than 1 and the number itself? _____

11. How many numbers between 1 and 10 have factors other than 1 and the number itself? _____

Module 1: Section D, Lesson 9

Name _____

Identify whether each number is prime or composite.

1. 3 _____   2. 7 _____

3. 2 _____   4. 8 _____

5. 16 _____   6. 1 _____

7. 21 _____   8. 22 _____

9. 23 _____   10. 9 _____

11. 11 _____   12. 31 _____

13. Draw as many arrays as you can for the number 12.

14. Draw as many arrays as you can for the number 25.

15. How many arrays can be made for a prime number?

_____

Module 1: Section D, Lesson 9

Name _____

Write the factors of the number. Then make a sketch of all the arrays of the number.

1. 13 _____

2. 10 _____

3. 14 _____

4. 18 _____

5. What are the prime numbers between 1 and 20? _____

6. What are the prime numbers between 21 and 40? _____

Divide.

7. $8\overline{)48}$

8. $7\overline{)56}$

9. $3\overline{)81}$

Module 1: Section D, Lesson 9

Name _____

1. Draw an array with 12 squares.

2. List the other arrays that can be made of 12 squares. List all the factors of 12.

   _____

3. Draw an array with 9 squares.

4. List all the arrays of 9 squares.
   What are the factors of 9? _____

5. Draw an array with 26 squares.

6. List all the arrays of 26 squares.
   What are the factors of 26? _____

Module 1: Section D, Lesson 9

Name _____

Materials: calculator

1. What is the first prime
   number after 50? _____

2. Write a plan for finding out whether 157
   is a prime or composite number. _____

   _____

   _____

Is each number prime?

3. 97 _____   4. 117 _____   5. 198 _____

6. 169 _____   7. 108 _____   8. 189 _____

9. Are there more prime numbers between
   1 and 100 or between 100 and 200? _____

   Why? _____

10. Do you think anyone can find the greatest
    prime number? Why or why not? _____

    _____

Module 1: Section D, Lesson 9   © Houghton Mifflin Company. All rights reserved/5

Name _____

Read each number. Identify the period, place, and value for the underlined digit.

SKILL
33
WORKSHEET

	period	place	value
1. 1,4<u>6</u>2	_____	_____	_____
2. <u>7</u>89	_____	_____	_____
3. <u>5</u>2,987	_____	_____	_____
4. <u>9</u>,453	_____	_____	_____
5. 3,6<u>0</u>9	_____	_____	_____
6. 4,<u>1</u>88	_____	_____	_____
7. <u>2</u>4,210	_____	_____	_____
8. <u>1</u>13, 465	_____	_____	_____
9. 89<u>9</u>	_____	_____	_____
10. 8,<u>7</u>62	_____	_____	_____
11. <u>5</u>65, 421	_____	_____	_____
12. <u>9</u>9,877	_____	_____	_____

Module 2: Section A, Lesson 1

Name _____

Write in standard form.

1. five hundred eighty-three _____

2. eleven thousand, three
   hundred twenty-four _____

3. six thousand, four hundred eleven _____

4. thirty-seven thousand,
   nine hundred twenty-six _____

5. fifty-one thousand _____

6. one hundred fifty-one
   thousand, eight hundred fifteen _____

7. two thousand eleven _____

8. six thousand, six hundred sixty-six _____

9. five hundred thirteen
   thousand, two hundred five _____

10. eighty-six thousand,
    nine hundred fourteen _____

Module 2: Section A, Lesson 1

Name _____

Write in word form.

1. 461 _____

2. 808 _____

3. 1,243 _____

4. 5,555 _____

5. 32,891 _____

6. 79,862,498 _____

_____

7. 642,194 _____

8. 1,111,111 _____

_____

9. 12,121,121 _____

_____

10. 1,234,567,890 _____

_____

Module 2: Section A, Lesson 1

Name _____

Write each number in at least two ways.

1. four hundred thirty-one

   a. _____   b. _____

2. three thousand, two hundred sixty-eight

   a. _____   b. _____

3. eighty thousand, five hundred twenty-one

   a. _____   b. _____

4. 67,699

   a. _____   b. _____

5. 1,357,924

   a. _____   b. _____

6. fifteen thousand, fifteen

   a. _____   b. _____

7. four hundred sixty-five thousand, sixty-five

   a. _____   b. _____

Module 2: Section A, Lesson 1

Name _____

Order from least to greatest. What places did you have to compare?

1. 311   301   310

_____

2. 1,008   1,088   1,080   1,018

_____

3. 26,266   26,260   26,206   26,226

_____

4. $6,586 $6,660 $6,606 $6,568

_____

5. 4,495   4, 459   4,559   4,549

_____

6. 3,737   3,773   3,373   3,377

_____

Module 2: Section A, Lesson 1

Name _____

Use the digits **1, 3, 5**, and **7** once each
to write the following numbers.

1. the least possible number _____

2. the greatest possible number _____

3. a number greater than 3,517 _____

4. a number less than 5,173 _____

5. a number greater than
1,753 but less than 7,153 _____

6. a number greater than
3,157 but less than 5,137 _____

7. five numbers greater than 3,571 _____

_____

8. five numbers less than 5,713 _____

_____

9. a number between 7,135 and 7,531 _____

10. a number between 1,375 and 1,573 _____

Name _____

Order from greatest to least.

1. 6,789   6,879   6,978   6,897

---

2. 2,431   3,124   3,214   2,341

---

3. 6,709   6,079   6,097   6,970

---

4. 24,682   22,468   22,864   24,826

---

5. 5,678   6,587   5,876   6,857

---

6. 31,597   31,975   13,579   13,759

Module 2: Section A, Lesson 2

Name _____

Order from least to greatest.

1. 8,321   8,213   8,123   8,312

_____

2. 5,454   5,445   4,455   4,554

_____

3. 19,767   19,776   19,677   17,976

_____

4. 32,289   32,829   32,982   32,892

_____

5. 205,205   205,052   225,005   225,500

_____

6. 7,361   7,631   6,137   6,716

_____

Module 2: Section A, Lesson 2

Name _____

Round to the underlined place.

1. <u>4</u>,706 _____

2. 61,1<u>2</u>9 _____

3. 2<u>3</u>6,589 _____

4. 13,<u>8</u>42 _____

5. 1<u>4</u>5,145,145 _____

6. 2<u>4</u>,873,324 _____

7. 8,<u>6</u>57 _____

8. 897,<u>7</u>655 _____

9. 46,<u>6</u>354 _____

10. 10<u>3</u>,476 _____

11. 11,<u>0</u>51 _____

12. 9,9<u>9</u>9 _____

Module 2: Section B, Lesson 3

Name _____

Round the number **35,167,384,507** to the indicated place.

1. hundreds _____

2. ten thousands _____

3. tens _____

4. hundred thousands _____

5. ten millions _____

6. millions _____

7. thousands _____

8. hundred millions _____

9. billions _____

10. ten billions _____

11. A number rounded to the nearest million is 11,000,000.

    a. What is the least number it could be? _____

    b. the greatest number it could be? _____

Module 2: Section B, Lesson 3

Name _____

Use mental math to find *n*.

1. $7 \times 10 = n$

_____

2. $10 \times n = 120$

_____

3. $n \times 10 = 280$

_____

4. $19 \times 10 = n$

_____

5. $n \times 10 = 320$

_____

6. $n \times 10 = 500$

_____

7. $20 \times 10 = n$

_____

8. $10 \times 11 = n$

_____

9. $10 \times n = 450$

_____

10. $10 \times n = 250$

_____

11. $10 \times 16 = n$

_____

12. $10 \times 61 = n$

_____

Module 2: Section B, Lesson 4

Name _____

Write each product in two other ways.

1. 8 × 10   _____   _____

2. (3 × 4) × 10   _____   _____

3. (5 × 5) × 10   _____   _____

4. (2 × 5) × 8   _____   _____

5. 24 × 10   _____   _____

6. (8 × 3) × 10   _____   _____

7. (7 × 6) × 10   _____   _____

8. 6 × 10   _____   _____

9. (8 × 8) × 10   _____   _____

10. (9 × 2) × 10   _____   _____

11. 56 × 10   _____   _____

12. (6 × 8) × 10   _____   _____

Module 2: Section B, Lesson 4

Name _____

Use mental math and the Associative Property of Multiplication to find the product.

1. $(6 \times 3) \times 10$

2. $10 \times (5 \times 7)$

3. $(5 \times 2) \times 8$

_____

4. $(8 \times 9) \times 10$

5. $17 \times (2 \times 5)$

6. $10 \times (3 \times 8)$

_____

7. $10 \times (5 \times 9)$

8. $(4 \times 5) \times 10$

9. $(7 \times 5) \times 10$

_____

10. $(2 \times 5) \times 16$

11. $10 \times (4 \times 9)$

12. $10 \times (6 \times 7)$

_____

13. $(8 \times 4) \times 10$

14. $(2 \times 5) \times 10$

15. $21 \times (5 \times 2)$

_____

16. $(18 \times 5) \times 2$

17. $(49 \times 2) \times 5$

18. $7 \times (8 \times 10)$

_____

Module 2: Section B, Lesson 4

Name _____

Use the Associative Property to write a different addition sentence. Then find the sum.

1. $(6 + 4) + 8$ _____ = _____

2. $1 + (9 + 7)$ _____ = _____

3. $(5 + 3) + 7$ _____ = _____

4. $(16 + 10) + 4$ _____ = _____

5. $20 + (10 + 32)$ _____ = _____

6. $28 + (17 + 3) + 2$ _____ = _____

7. $(25 + 5) + 15 + 5$ _____ = _____

8. $26 + (14 + 6)$ _____ = _____

9. $(23 + 24) + 61 + 9$ _____ = _____

10. $(31 + 27) + 33$ _____ = _____

11. $22 + 18 + (14 + 12)$ _____ = _____

12. $24 + (36 + 29)$ _____ = _____

Module 2: Section B, Lesson 4

Name _____

Rewrite the multiplication sentence using the Associative or Commutative Property. Then find the product.

1. 10 × 30

_____

2. 10 × 16

_____

3. 20 × 18

_____

4. 40 × 15

_____

5. 10 × 60

_____

6. 10 × 15

_____

7. 18 × 30

_____

8. 60 × 80

_____

9. 14 × 40

_____

10. 50 × 29

_____

11. 30 × 16

_____

12. 100 × 100

_____

Name _____

Use the following list of time periods to answer the questions below.

1 year = 365 days
1 day = 24 hours
1 hour = 60 minutes
1 minute = 60 seconds

1. How many hours are in 20 days? _____

2. How many seconds are in 30 minutes? _____

3. How many days are in 40 years? _____

4. How many minutes are in 50 hours? _____

5. How many seconds are in 60 minutes? _____

6. How many seconds are in a day? _____

7. How many seconds are in a week? _____

8. How many seconds are in 4 weeks? _____

9. How many seconds are in a year? _____

10. How many seconds are in 10 years? _____

Module 2: Section B, Lesson 5

Name _____

Find the area and perimeter for rectangles with a width of 4 ft and with these lengths.

1. 5 ft $A =$ _____ $P =$ _____

2. 6 ft $A =$ _____ $P =$ _____

3. 7 ft $A =$ _____ $P =$ _____

4. 8 ft $A =$ _____ $P =$ _____

5. 9 ft $A =$ _____ $P =$ _____

6. 10 ft $A =$ _____ $P =$ _____

7. 15 ft $A =$ _____ $P =$ _____

8. 20 ft $A =$ _____ $P =$ _____

9. 25 ft $A =$ _____ $P =$ _____

10. 30 ft $A =$ _____ $P =$ _____

Module 2: Section C, Lesson 6

Name _____

Substitute the given values in each
expression. Then solve.

Area = $l \times w$

1. $l = 7$ ft; $w = 8$ ft $A =$ _____

2. $l = 12$ ft; $w = 10$ ft $A =$ _____

3. $l = 24$ ft; $w = 30$ ft $A =$ _____

Area = s^2

4. $s = 9$ $A =$ _____

5. $s = 11$ $A =$ _____

6. $s = 20$ $A =$ _____

Perimeter = $2(l + w)$

7. $l = 3$ ft; $w = 7$ ft $P =$ _____

8. $l = 14$ ft; $w = 4$ ft $P =$ _____

9. $l = 15$ ft; $w = 15$ ft $P =$ _____

Module 2: Section C, Lesson 6

Name _____

Use exponents to write the following numbers.

1. $2 \times 2 \times 2$

2. 5×5

3. $6 \times 6 \times 6$

_____   _____   _____

4. $8 \times 8 \times 8 \times 8$

5. $1 \times 1 \times 1 \times 1$

6. 9×9

_____   _____   _____

7. $10 \times 10 \times 10$

8. 18×18

9. 3×3

_____   _____   _____

10. $12 \times 12 \times 12$

11. $10 \times 10 \times 10 \times 10$

_____   _____

12. 11×11

13. $4 \times 4 \times 4 \times 4 \times 4$

_____   _____

14. $7 \times 7 \times 7$

15. $100 \times 100 \times 100 \times 100$

_____   _____

Module 2: Section C, Lesson 6

Name _____

Write two-digit numbers, using the following four digits.

6, 9, 7, 4

1. List four possible two-digit numbers.

_____

2. Which combination gives you the greatest area?

_____

3. Which combination gives you the least area?

_____

4. Which combination gives you the greatest perimeter?

_____

5. Which combination gives you the least perimeter?

_____

Module 2: Section C, Lesson 6

Name _____

SKILL
53
WORKSHEET

Use the Distributive Property to help
you find the areas.

1. 20 ft × 30 ft _____

2. 16 ft × 18 ft _____

3. 26 ft × 14 ft _____

4. 81 ft × 20 ft _____

5. 36 ft × 72 ft _____

6. 25 ft × 51 ft _____

7. 44 ft × 32 ft _____

8. 28 ft × 56 ft _____

9. 12 ft × 62 ft _____

10. 11 ft × 86 ft _____

11. 35 ft × 26 ft _____

12. 27 ft × 21 ft _____

Module 2: Section C, Lesson 7

Name _____

Use the Distributive Property to help
you find the products.

1. 79 × 62 _____

2. 80 × 76 _____

3. 52 × 20 _____

4. 28 × 46 _____

5. 42 × 53 _____

6. 27 × 33 _____

7. 50 × 84 _____

8. 21 × 28 _____

9. 30 × 68 _____

10. 22 × 45 _____

11. 34 × 72 _____

12. 55 × 55 _____

Name _____

Estimate. If the estimate is greater than 500, find the exact product.

1. 19 × 12 _____

2. 35 × 11 _____

3. 36 × 80 _____

4. 24 × 16 _____

5. 39 × 17 _____

6. 21 × 51 _____

7. 15 × 18 _____

8. 25 × 27 _____

9. 41 × 22 _____

10. 13 × 33 _____

11. 28 × 46 _____

12. 23 × 48 _____

Module 2: Section C, Lesson 7

Name _____

Complete the number sentence for the given value of *n*. Then calculate.

1. $n = 3$ $12 \times (n + 4)$ _____

2. $n = 1$ $n \times (n + 15)$ _____

3. $n = 2$ $n^2 + (n + 9)$ _____

4. $n = 6$ $14 \times (n + 14)$ _____

5. $n = 4$ $(16 + 24) \times n$ _____

6. $n = 5$ $n \times (25 + n)$ _____

7. $n = 2$ $30 \times (n + 4)$ _____

8. $n = 4$ $6 \times n \times (n + 6)$ _____

9. $n = 3$ $12 \times n^2$ _____

10. $n = 5$ $n \times n \times n$ _____

11. $n = 1$ $n \times (37 + 29)$ _____

12. $n = 6$ $(8 \times n) + 2$ _____

Module 2: Section C, Lesson 7

Name _____

Find the average.

SKILL 57 WORKSHEET

1. 5, 7, 8, 11, 4

2. 30, 11, 14, 17

_____

_____

3. $37, $55, $85

4. 140, 265, 558

_____

_____

5. $35, $37, $54, $62

6. 81 + 82 + 83 + 84 + 85

_____

_____

7. 1, 2, 3, 4, 5,

8. 100, 101, 102

_____

_____

9. 41, 137, 20, 106, 176

10. 7, 5, 15, 8, 10

_____

_____

Name _____

Write two sets of three different numbers whose average is given.

1. 9 _____ _____ _____

         _____ _____ _____

2. 12 _____ _____ _____

         _____ _____ _____

3. 5 _____ _____ _____

         _____ _____ _____

4. 24 _____ _____ _____

         _____ _____ _____

5. $18 _____ _____ _____

         _____ _____ _____

Module 2: Section D, Lesson 8

Name _____

Calculate. Then write an equation showing the inverse operation.

1. $54 + 99 =$ _____   _____

2. $34 - 18 =$ _____   _____

3. $73 - 51 =$ _____   _____

4. $23 + 48 =$ _____   _____

5. $66 + 13 =$ _____   _____

6. $82 + 57 =$ _____   _____

7. $98 - 59 =$ _____   _____

8. $103 - 35 =$ _____   _____

9. $26 + 16 =$ _____   _____

10. $92 - 56 =$ _____   _____

11. $101 - 47 =$ _____   _____

12. $81 - 32 =$ _____   _____

13. $29 + 62 =$ _____   _____

Module 2: Section D, Lesson 8

Name _____

Calculate. Then write an equation showing the inverse operation.

1. $8 \times 4 =$ _____   _____

2. $53 - 18 =$ _____   _____

3. $8 \times 5 =$ _____   _____

4. $28 + 39 =$ _____   _____

5. $44 + 67 =$ _____   _____

6. $0 \div 9 =$ _____   _____

7. $19 \times 9 =$ _____   _____

8. $101 - 75 =$ _____   _____

9. $36 + 58 =$ _____   _____

10. $90 - 42 =$ _____   _____

11. $0 \div 47 =$ _____   _____

12. $7 \times 8 =$ _____   _____

13. $12 \times 13 =$ _____   _____

Module 2: Section D, Lesson 8

Name _____

Write the number of places in the quotient. Then find the quotient.

1. 9)25

2. 8)432

_____   _____

3. 6)512

4. 4)60

_____   _____

5. 5)50

6. 7)290

_____   _____

7. 8)373

8. 2)75

_____   _____

9. 3)244

10. 9)852

_____   _____

Module 2: Section D, Lesson 9

Name _____

Estimate the quotient. If the estimate is greater than 50, find the exact quotient.

1. 8)82

_____

2. 4)220

_____

3. 7)559

_____

4. 8)478

_____

5. 6)536

_____

6. 3)265

_____

7. 5)332

_____

8. 2)111

_____

9. 9)626

_____

10. 3)208

_____

Name _____

Find the quotient.

1. $8\overline{)84}$ 2. $4\overline{)317}$

3. $6\overline{)95}$ 4. $3\overline{)115}$

5. $4\overline{)206}$ 6. $5\overline{)435}$

7. $8\overline{)284}$ 8. $6\overline{)372}$

9. $9\overline{)159}$ 10. $7\overline{)564}$

11. $2\overline{)87}$ 12. $9\overline{)386}$

Module 2: Section D, Lesson 9

Name _____

Divide each number by two different divisors that produce quotients with no remainders.

1. 10   _____   _____

2. 20   _____   _____

3. 30   _____   _____

4. 40   _____   _____

5. 50   _____   _____

6. 60   _____   _____

7. 70   _____   _____

8. 80   _____   _____

9. 90   _____   _____

10. 100   _____   _____

11. 24   _____   _____

12. 36   _____   _____

Module 2: Section D, Lesson 9

Name _____

Solve.

1. A CD costs $12.29. You give the salesperson $15.00. What coin or coins should you get back in change? _____

2. A book has 25 stamps. Each stamp costs $0.29. If you buy a book, how much change will you get back from $8.00? _____

3. You visit a baseball card booth at a flea market. You buy 5 cards at $0.10 each and 3 cards at $0.16 each. How much change will you get back from a one dollar bill? _____

4. At the supermarket, you buy 1 pound of apples for $1.29, and 1 dozen oranges for $0.99. How much change in coins will you get back from $3.00? _____

Module 3: Section A, Lesson 1

Name _____

Solve.

1. A book costs $3.98. You give the salesperson $5.00. What coin or coins should you get back in change?

_____

2. Flowers cost $4 a bunch. You buy 6 bunches. How much change will
you get back from $25.00? _____

You go to a garage sale and buy three board games that cost $2 each and six pens that cost $0.25 each.

3. How much change will you
get from a ten dollar bill? _____

4. You have $35. If computer games cost $30 each, how many board games, pens, and computer games can you buy if you want to buy at least one of each, and if you want to spend all the money?

_____

Module 3: Section A, Lesson 1

Name _____

Estimate totals by rounding and by front-end estimation.

1. Groceries: bread $1.29, eggs $0.99, coffee $2.49, milk $1.19

   _____

2. Greeting cards: for Mom $1.25, for Dad $1.60, for sister $1.35

   _____

3. Party favors: confetti $3.50, streamers $1.75, hats $4.00, paper plates $3.25, paper cups $3.25, tablecloth $2.49

   _____

4. Fruit: A pound of pears $1.29, a pound of cherries $2.59, cantaloupe $1.79, 3 pounds of bananas $1.00

   _____

Module 3: Section A, Lesson 2

Name _____

Estimate totals by rounding and by front-end estimation.

1. $5.70, $4.19, $0.63   _____

2. $2.53, $1.42, $4.98   _____

3. $1.39, $2.49, $4.10   _____

4. $5.89, $3.19, $1.49   _____

5. $7.19, $1.29, $2.58, $2.49   _____

6. $1.59, $6.08, $3.79, $2.19   _____

7. Which kind of estimating do you find most helpful, rounding to the nearest dollar or front-end estimation? Why?

_____

8. When should you use rounding?

_____

9. When should you use front-end estimation?

_____

Module 3: Section A, Lesson 2

Name _____

Complete the charts.

1.

Amount	Divided by	How many?
200	10	20
400	10	
800	10	
1,000	10	
1,200	10	

2.

Amount	Divided by	How many?
600	30	20
1,200	30	
1,800	30	
2,400	30	

3.

Amount	Divided by	How many?
100	50	
1,000	50	
10,000	50	
20,000	50	
50,000	50	

4.

Amount	Divided by	How many?
2,000	20	
4,000	20	
4,000	40	
8,000	40	
16,000	40	

Module 3: Section A, Lesson 3

Name _____

Divide.

1. $20\overline{)220}$ **2.** $10\overline{)180}$ **3.** $50\overline{)150}$

4. $30\overline{)120}$ **5.** $70\overline{)630}$ **6.** $80\overline{)320}$

7. $40\overline{)3,600}$ **8.** $90\overline{)2,700}$ **9.** $40\overline{)9,200}$

10. Complete the chart. Do you see a pattern?

Amount	Divided by	How many?
90	30	
450	30	
2,250	30	

_____

_____

_____

_____

Module 3: Section A, Lesson 3

Name _____

Divide.

1. $10\overline{)440}$ 2. $40\overline{)320}$ 3. $20\overline{)280}$

4. $60\overline{)2,400}$ 5. $70\overline{)4,200}$ 6. $60\overline{)18,000}$

7. $80\overline{)72,800}$ 8. $70\overline{)36,200}$ 9. $40\overline{)52,400}$

Solve.

10. Shayla's class wants to buy pizzas for a class
     party. If the pizzas cost $10.00 each, how many
     pizzas can they buy for $200.00?

     _____

Module 3: Section A, Lesson 3

Name _____

Divide.

1. 30)2,100   **2.** 20)1,600   **3.** 40)8,000

4. 50)5,000   **5.** 30)33,000   **6.** 20)82,000

7. If you know that 60)3,000 is 50,
how can you find 60)30,000? _____

8. If you know that 70)4,900 is 70,
how can you find 70)49,000? _____

9. If you know that 30)300 is 10, how can you find
30)30,000 ? How can you find 30)60,000?

_____

10. Jackie has $500.00 in $10 dollar bills,
how many $10 bills does she have? _____

Module 3: Section A, Lesson 3

Name _____

Circle the correct answer.

1. Is cheese sold by weight or capacity?

2. Are potatoes sold by weight or capacity?

3. Is vinegar sold by weight or capacity?

4. Is laundry detergent sold by weight or capacity?

Convert.

5. 20 oz = _____ lb _____ oz

6. 6 qt = _____ gal _____ qt

7. 5 c = _____ qt _____ c

8. 40 oz = _____ lb _____ oz

9. 64 fl oz = _____ qt

10. 16 pt = _____ gal

11. How many pints are in 1 quart? _____

12. How many fluid ounces are in 1 quart? _____

Module 3: Section B, Lesson 4

Name _____

Convert each amount to the next smallest unit. Name the units when you can convert to different smaller units.

1 1.5 lb _____

2. 0.5 gal _____

3. 3 c _____

Convert each amount to the next largest unit. Name the units when you can convert to different larger units.

4. 11 c _____

5. 72 fl oz _____

6. 64 oz _____

7. How many cups are in 1 quart? _____

8. How many fluid ounces are in a gallon? _____

9. What is the difference between weight and capacity?

_____

_____

Module 3: Section B, Lesson 4

Name _____

How many digits are in each quotient?

1. $38\overline{)359}$ _____ 2. $66\overline{)501}$ _____

3. $46\overline{)989}$ _____ 4. $39\overline{)675}$ _____

5. $97\overline{)872}$ _____ 6. $71\overline{)1,236}$ _____

Estimate the quotients. Use guess and check to solve.

7. $31\overline{)124}$ 8. $54\overline{)486}$ 9. $41\overline{)287}$

10. Jed spends $6.86 to buy the ingredients to make cookies for the bake sale. If he can make 8 dozen cookies, estimate how much it costs per cookie.

_____

Module 3: Section B, Lesson 5

Name _____

Estimate the quotients.

1. $42\overline{)675}$ **2.** $33\overline{)756}$ **3.** $88\overline{)916}$

4. $23\overline{)356}$ **5.** $52\overline{)639}$ **6.** $79\overline{)448}$

Estimate how many quarters are in the amount.

7. $5.80   **8.** $11.78   **9.** $9.67

_____   _____   _____

10. $5.45   **11.** $8.75   **12.** $6.90

_____   _____   _____

13. Explain how you found your estimates to these exercises. Did your estimates improve as you did more exercises?

_____

Module 3: Section B, Lesson 5

Name _____

Jennie's class of 32 students is planning to make frozen yogurt sundaes. Here is what they will pay for the items they need.

Frozen Yogurt	1 gallon	32 servings	$6.72
Sprinkles	1 pound	32 servings	$3.20
Hot Fudge	2 quarts	32 servings	$6.40
Cherries	8 ounces	32 servings	$1.60

Find the price per serving for each item.

1. Frozen Yogurt _____   **2.** Sprinkles _____

3. Hot Fudge _____   **4.** Cherries _____

5. What is the most expensive item per serving? _____

6. What is the least expensive item per serving? _____

7. What is the total cost per student? _____

Module 3: Section B, Lesson 5

Name _____

Martha and her 3 friends are planning to make Halloween costumes with these materials.

Item	Number of Pieces	Amount per Piece	Total Cost
Cloth	4	2 yd.	$4.20
Paper	4	1 lb.	$2.80
Trim	4	4 yd.	$3.20

Find the price per piece for each item.

1. Cloth _____ **2.** Paper _____ **3.** Trim _____

4. What is the most expensive item per piece? _____

5. What is the least expensive item per piece? _____

6. What is the total cost per child? _____

7. What is the total cost for the children? _____

Name _____

Find the unit price.

1. 8 lb for $8.98 _____ **2.** 7 lb for $7.49 _____

3. 1 qt for $0.79 _____ **4.** 3 qt for $3.00 _____

5. 3 jars for $2.89 _____ **6.** 4 jars for $3.49 _____

7. 5 yd for $4.00 _____ **8.** 7 yd for $6.69 _____

9. 16 oz for $3.20 _____ **10.** 24 oz for $4.32 _____

11. 9 lb for $3.24 _____ **12.** 6 cans for $2.70 _____

Module 3: Section B, Lesson 6

Name _____

Find the unit price for each pair. Then circle the best buy.

1. 1 gal for $0.99 _____   10 gal for $8.00 _____

2. 5 sticks for $0.25 _____   8 sticks for $0.32 _____

3. 10 bars for $1.00 _____   6 bars for $.90 _____

4. 2 dozen for $1.44 _____   5 dozen for $3.00 _____

5. 24 fl oz for $2.40 _____   8 fl oz for $.96 _____

6. 12 ft at $1.92 _____   6 ft at $1.08 _____

7. What other factors, besides unit price, should you consider when choosing the best buy?

_____

Solve.

8. Jose's mother sent you to the store for paper towels. Squeezies are 3 rolls for $1.80, WipeUps 5 rolls for $3.00, and MopDries 8 rolls for $4.00. Which brand is the best buy? _____

Module 3: Section B, Lesson 6

Name _____

If the quotient has an error, correct it.
Write C if the quotient is correct.

1. $\overline{126}$ R5
     $8)\overline{1,012}$

2. $\overline{119}$
     $5)\overline{995}$

3. $\overline{561}$ R1
     $6)\overline{3,336}$

4. $\overline{301}$ R4
     $7)\overline{2,174}$

Solve for *n*.

5. $27 + 32 = n$

   $n =$ _____

6. $14 - 3 = n$

   $n =$ _____

7. $72 \times 10 = n$

   $n =$ _____

8. $53 + 19 = n$

   $n =$ _____

Module 3: Section C, Lesson 7

Name _____

Some of these exercises have errors. Fix any errors. Write C if the quotient is correct.

1. $\overset{415 \text{ R1}}{3)\overline{1{,}235}}$

2. $\overset{388 \text{ R4}}{9)\overline{3{,}496}}$

3. $\overset{738}{6)\overline{4{,}428}}$

4. $\overset{790}{5)\overline{3{,}545}}$

Solve for n.

5. $98 - 56 = n$

$n = $ _____

6. $22 \times 15 = n$

$n = $ _____

7. $83 + 27 = n$

$n = $ _____

8. $128 - 57 = n$

$n = $ _____

Module 3: Section C, Lesson 7

Name _____

Estimate the first digit in each quotient.
Check your estimate by multiplying.

1. 5)25

2. 5)2,500

3. 5)2,538

4. 25)2,538

5. 50)2,500

6. 50)2,535

7. 60)4,200

8. 60)4,277

9. Can you share 22 one hundred dollar bills among 16 people? How many will each person get? How many will be left?

_____

Module 3: Section C, Lesson 8

Name _____

Estimate the first digit in each quotient.
Check your estimate by multiplying.

1. 22)6,662

2. 27)7,890

3. 15)6,049

4. 18)9,451

5. 50)1,536

6. 57)3,389

7. 25)4,275

8. 46)7,831

9. 56)2,593

10. 21)4,473

11. How many pounds are 6,400 oz? _____

Name _____

Finish the division.

1. $3\square$
    $41\overline{)1,556}$
    $-1\,23$

2. $5\square$
    $63\overline{)3,463}$
    -3

3. $3\square$
    $28\overline{)885}$
    -8

4. $1\square$
    $57\overline{)1,009}$
    $-\,57$

5. $2\square$
    $93\overline{)1,959}$
    $-1\,86$

6. $9\square$
    $75\overline{)6,924}$
    $-6\,75$

7. $7\square$
    $78\overline{)6,059}$
    $-5\,66$

8. $7\square$
    $23\overline{)1,659}$
    $-1\,66$

Name _____

Estimate the first digit by using numbers that are easy to divide. Check your estimates with your calculator.

1. 27)5,063

2. 58)1,206

3. 64)13,000

4. 78)25,343

Round the divisor to estimate the first digit.

5. 38)4,400

6. 84)1,685

Write an explanation of the method you would use to estimate the first digit of the quotient. Find the first digit.

7. 62)2,345

8. 99)2,020

_____   _____

Module 3: Section C, Lesson 8   © Houghton Mifflin Company. All rights reserved/5

Name _____

Answer the questions below.

1. What place will be the first
   digit in the quotient 14)860 ?

   _____

2. To solve 14)860 , trade the hundreds in for tens.
   How many tens will you have? Explain the next
   step in the division. What is the result?

   _____

3. Explain the next step of the solution to 14)860 .
   What is the result? What is the quotient?

   _____

   _____

4. To solve 47)945 , trade the hundreds in for tens.
   How many tens will you have? Explain the next
   step in the division. What is the result?

   _____

   _____

Module 3: Section C, Lesson 9

Name _____

Divide.

1. $12 \overline{)252}$ 2. $18 \overline{)450}$ 3. $23 \overline{)1,012}$

4. $56 \overline{)1,064}$ 5. $48 \overline{)1,253}$ 6. $38 \overline{)657}$

7. $90 \overline{)1,629}$ 8. $74 \overline{)1,944}$ 9. $77 \overline{)2,701}$

10. If the remainder in your quotient is larger than your divisor, what should you do?

_____

Module 3: Section C, Lesson 9

Name _____

Here is some data from a city about drinking milk.

Age Group	Number of fl oz per day
Children under 13	16
Children 13–20	10
Adults 21–49	8
Adults over 49	12

1. Make a bar graph from the data in the table.

2. What does the vertical axis show? _____

3. What does the horizontal axis show? _____

4. Which group drinks the most amount of milk? _____

5. In general, do children or adults drink more milk? How can you tell?

_____

Name _____

The bar graph below shows the number of books published by subject in the United States in 1990.

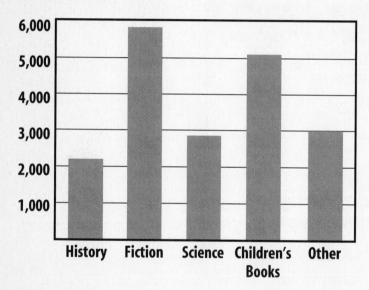

1. What does the horizontal axis show? _____

2. What does the vertical axis show? _____

3. Which of these subjects had the most books published? _____

Module 3: Section D, Lesson 10

Name _____

This double-bar graph shows how much was produced in the United States in 1985 and 1989. Use the graph to answer the questions.

1. Which product had the highest total production in 1985? (in 1989?)

   _____

   _____

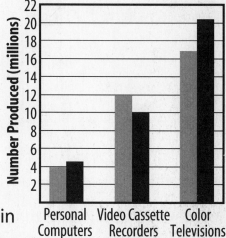

2. Look at the changes in production between 1985 and 1989. For which products did production increase? _____

   decrease? _____

3. Which product had the highest increase in production between 1985 and 1989?

   _____

Module 3: Section D, Lesson 11

Name _____

SKILL
WORKSHEET
92

Here is some data from a city about drinking milk.

Age Group	Number of fl oz per day
Children under 13	16
Children 13–18	10
Adults 19–49	8
Adults over 49	12

1. Make a pictograph from the data in the table.

2. What is the scale you used for the data? _____

3. Which group drinks three-quarters of the amount that children under 13 drink?

    _____

4. Which group drinks half the amount that children under 13 drink?

    _____

5. For this data which type of graph is easier to read, the bar graph or the pictograph? Why?

    _____

Module 3: Section D, Lesson 11

Name _____

This double-bar graph shows the sales of vehicles in the United States in 1985 and 1990. Use the graph to answer the questions.

1. Which vehicle had the most sales in

   1985? _____

   1990? _____

2. Which vehicle had the least sales in

   1985? _____

   1990? _____

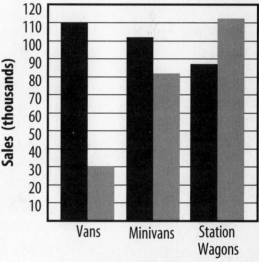

3. Which vehicle increased in sales between 1985 and 1990? _____

4. About how much did the sales of minivans decrease between 1985 and 1990?

   _____

Module 3: Section D, Lesson 11

Name _____

This double-bar graph shows the sales of breakfast cereals in 1985 and 1990. Use the graph to answer the questions.

1. Which breakfast cereal had the most sales in

   1985? _____

   1990? _____

2. Which breakfast cereal had the least sales in

   1985? _____

   1990? _____

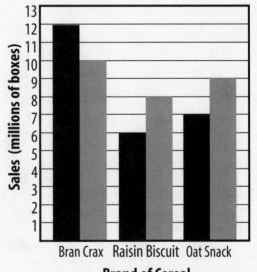

3. Which breakfast cereal increased in sales between 1985 and 1990? _____

4. About how much did the sales of Oat Snack increase between 1985 and 1990? _____

Module 3: Section D, Lesson 11

Name _____

Use the chart to decide on which show the company should advertise its products.

Type of Show	Number of Viewers	$ Per Minute
Cartoons	2,100,000	$175,000
Music Videos	3,700,000	$ 30,500
Family Comedy	8,600,000	$106,400
Sports Weekend	3,400,000	$750,000

1. RocknRoll Inc. sells tapes of hard to find "oldies."

_____

2. CrunchMaster sells a low fat and low sugar corn snack.

_____

3. Jump Higher sells a new kind of sports shoe. _____

4. NothingDoing sells unusual toys. _____

5. Which show costs the most per ad? (the least?)

   the most _____ the least _____

6. Who would be the audience for each show?_____

Module 3: Section D, Lesson 12

Name _____

Use the chart to decide which publication the company should advertise its products in.

Publication	Number of Subscribers	Cost Per Ad
Sport Bimonthly	115,000	$16,000
Local Newspaper	77,000	$ 3,500
Her Magazine	368,000	$23,000
Business Weekly	257,000	$19,500

1. Hotsport makes running shoes.

   _____

2. Pursemaker sells woman's hand bags.

   _____

3. Manswear makes men's suits. _____

4. Tritown Auto Sales is a car dealer. _____

5. Which two publications reach the greatest number of people? _____

6. Which publication costs the most per ad? (the least)

   the most _____ the least _____

Module 3: Section D, Lesson 12

Name _____

Draw the whole if the square equals the part given: ☐. Shade the part given.

1. $\frac{1}{2}$ of a rectangle

2. $\frac{1}{4}$ of a larger square

3. $\frac{2}{3}$ of a rectangle

4. $\frac{1}{3}$ of a rectangle

5. Name the fraction of the whole that is not shaded in Exercises 1–4.

_____

Module 4: Section A, Lesson 1

Name _____

Draw a shape and shade it to show these fractions:

1. $\frac{5}{8}$

2. $\frac{3}{4}$

3. $\frac{9}{10}$

4. $\frac{1}{6}$

5. Name the fraction of the whole that is not shaded in Exercises 1–4.

_____

Module 4: Section A, Lesson 1

Name _____

Find the sum or difference.

1. $\frac{1}{7} + \frac{4}{7} = \frac{\boxed{}}{\boxed{}}$

2. $\frac{3}{5} - \frac{2}{5} = \frac{\boxed{}}{\boxed{}}$

3. $\frac{5}{9} + \frac{2}{9} = \frac{\boxed{}}{\boxed{}}$

4. $\frac{7}{16} - \frac{3}{16} = \frac{\boxed{}}{\boxed{}}$

5. $\frac{9}{10} - \frac{2}{10} = \frac{\boxed{}}{\boxed{}}$

6. $\frac{1}{3} + \frac{1}{3} = \frac{\boxed{}}{\boxed{}}$

Find the sum or difference. Write your answer in words.

7. Two sixths + three sixths = _____

8. Nine twelfths – four twelfths = _____

9. Five eighths + two eighths = _____

10. Eight ninths – one ninth = _____

11. Seven sixteenths – six sixteenths =

_____

Module 4: Section A, Lesson 1

Name _____

Find the missing fraction.

1. $\frac{1}{3} + \dfrac{\boxed{}}{\boxed{}} = \frac{3}{3}$

2. $\frac{2}{5} + \dfrac{\boxed{}}{\boxed{}} = \frac{5}{5}$

3. $\frac{7}{12} + \dfrac{\boxed{}}{\boxed{}} = \frac{12}{12}$

4. $\frac{6}{10} + \dfrac{\boxed{}}{\boxed{}} = \frac{10}{10}$

5. $\dfrac{\boxed{}}{\boxed{}} + \frac{14}{20} = \frac{20}{20}$

6. $\dfrac{\boxed{}}{\boxed{}} + \frac{7}{18} = \frac{18}{18}$

7. $\dfrac{\boxed{}}{\boxed{}} + \frac{9}{15} = \frac{15}{15}$

8. $\dfrac{\boxed{}}{\boxed{}} + \frac{2}{8} = \frac{8}{8}$

9. $\dfrac{\boxed{}}{\boxed{}} + \frac{3}{16} = \frac{11}{16}$

10. $\frac{12}{24} + \dfrac{\boxed{}}{\boxed{}} = \frac{21}{24}$

Module 4: Section A, Lesson 1

Name _____

1. Circle the fractions that are equivalent to $\frac{2}{3}$.

$\frac{6}{9}$ $\qquad$ $\frac{12}{15}$ $\qquad$ $\frac{6}{12}$ $\qquad$ $\frac{24}{36}$ $\qquad$ $\frac{10}{18}$ $\qquad$ $\frac{18}{30}$ $\qquad$ $\frac{4}{6}$ $\qquad$ $\frac{30}{45}$

Solve for n.

2. $6 + \frac{2}{3} = n$ _____

3. $\frac{1}{2} = \frac{n}{10}$ _____

4. $\frac{2}{7} + n = \frac{5}{7}$ _____

5. $8 + \frac{5}{8} = n$ _____

6. $\frac{10}{15} = \frac{2}{n}$ _____

7. $\frac{n}{6} = \frac{2}{3}$ _____

8. $\frac{6}{8} = \frac{3}{n}$ _____

9. $2 + \frac{2}{9} = n$ _____

10. $\frac{2}{9} + n = \frac{5}{9}$ _____

11. $1 + \frac{2}{3} = n$ _____

12. $\frac{1}{5} + \frac{2}{5} = n$ _____

13. $3 + \frac{3}{4} = n$ _____

Module 4: Section A, Lesson 2

Name _____

Fill in the blanks to find equivalent fractions.

1. $\dfrac{1}{2} = \dfrac{\square}{4} = \dfrac{3}{\square} = \dfrac{\square}{8} = \dfrac{5}{\square}$

2. $\dfrac{1}{3} = \dfrac{2}{\square} = \dfrac{\square}{9} = \dfrac{4}{\square} = \dfrac{\square}{15}$

3. $\dfrac{1}{4} = \dfrac{\square}{8} = \dfrac{3}{\square} = \dfrac{\square}{16} = \dfrac{5}{\square}$

Write one equivalent fraction with a greater denominator and one with a smaller denominator for each fraction below.

4. $\dfrac{2}{4}$ _____

5. $\dfrac{2}{8}$ _____

6. $\dfrac{2}{6}$ _____

7. $\dfrac{2}{20}$ _____

8. $\dfrac{9}{18}$ _____

9. $\dfrac{5}{25}$ _____

Module 4: Section A, Lesson 2

Name _____

Using the set of the 50 United States, write the fraction for:

1. Number of states beginning with W. _____

2. Number of states with at least one side touching the Atlantic Ocean. _____

3. Number of states which do not touch another state. _____

4. Number of states on the Great Lakes. _____

5. Number of states with a two-word name. _____

6. Number of states that touch the Mississippi River. _____

7. Number of states bordering Mexico. _____

8. Number of states that end in A. _____

9. Number of states with at least one side touching the Pacific Ocean. _____

10. Number of states beginning with M. _____

Module 4: Section A, Lesson 3

Name _____

What fraction of the rectangle has circles in it?

1.

2.

3.

_____   _____   _____

4.

5.

6.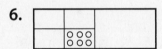

_____   _____   _____

7.

8.

9.

_____   _____   _____

Name _____

Estimate. Then solve for *n*.

	Estimate	Actual

1. $\frac{7}{8} \times 7 = n$ _____ _____

2. $\frac{4}{5} \times \frac{1}{2} = n$ _____ _____

3. $5 \times \frac{2}{3} = n$ _____ _____

4. $\frac{7}{10} \times 9 = n$ _____ _____

5. $8 \times \frac{5}{16} = n$ _____ _____

6. $\frac{3}{4} \times \frac{2}{9} = n$ _____ _____

7. $\frac{3}{4} \times \frac{1}{6} = n$ _____ _____

8. $\frac{2}{5} \times \frac{1}{3} = n$ _____ _____

9. $\frac{3}{8} \times \frac{1}{2} = n$ _____ _____

10. $\frac{5}{7} \times \frac{2}{9} = n$ _____ _____

11. $\frac{2}{3} \times \frac{1}{7} = n$ _____ _____

12. $\frac{5}{9} \times \frac{4}{3} = n$ _____ _____

Module 4: Section B, Lesson 4

Name _____

Fill in the table to increase or decrease the recipe.

Ginger Cookies	4 dozen	2 dozen	1 dozen	8 dozen
Butter	$\frac{1}{2}$ c	1.	11.	21.
Sugar	1 c	2.	12.	22.
Brown sugar	1 c	3.	13.	23.
Eggs	2	4.	14.	24.
Molasses	$\frac{1}{4}$ c	5.	15.	25.
Flour	2 c	6.	16.	26.
Baking powder	1 tsp	7.	17.	27.
Ginger	1 tsp	8.	18.	28.
Cinnamon	$\frac{1}{2}$ tsp	9.	19.	29.
Cloves	$\frac{1}{4}$ tsp	10.	20.	30.

Name _____

Multiply the following fractions. Draw an array to illustrate each solution.

1. $\frac{2}{3} \times \frac{2}{3}$

2. $\frac{2}{7} \times \frac{1}{6}$

3. $\frac{1}{2} \times \frac{5}{9}$

4. $\frac{3}{8} \times \frac{2}{6}$

5. $\frac{7}{8} \times \frac{1}{4}$

6. $\frac{2}{3} \times \frac{6}{10}$

Module 4: Section B, Lesson 5

Name _____

Multiply the following fractions. Draw an array to illustrate each solution.

1. $\frac{1}{3} \times \frac{3}{5}$

2. $\frac{3}{10} \times \frac{2}{3}$

3. $\frac{3}{4} \times \frac{7}{10}$

4. $\frac{4}{5} \times \frac{7}{9}$

5. $\frac{5}{6} \times \frac{9}{10}$

6. $\frac{2}{8} \times \frac{1}{2}$

Module 4: Section B, Lesson 5

Name _____

Use the Identity Property of Multiplication. Write three equivalent fractions.

1. $\frac{3}{7}$ _____ _____ _____

2. $\frac{1}{10}$ _____ _____ _____

3. $\frac{2}{3}$ _____ _____ _____

4. $\frac{4}{5}$ _____ _____ _____

5. $\frac{3}{9}$ _____ _____ _____

6. $\frac{1}{2}$ _____ _____ _____

7. $\frac{5}{6}$ _____ _____ _____

8. $\frac{5}{8}$ _____ _____ _____

9. $\frac{5}{11}$ _____ _____ _____

10. $\frac{3}{12}$ _____ _____ _____

11. $\frac{3}{4}$ _____ _____ _____

12. $\frac{7}{8}$ _____ _____ _____

Module 4: Section B, Lesson 6

Name _____

SKILL
110
WORKSHEET

Round these numbers to the
nearest 100.

1. 327   _____   **2.** 6,378   _____

3. 2,567   _____   **4.** 45,849   _____

5. 478,329 _____   **6.** 8,521,095 _____

7. 951   _____   **8.** 3,543   _____

Divide only exercises with quotients greater
than 100.

9. 18)‾2‾,‾0‾0‾0   **10.** 9)‾6‾4‾7   **11.** 27)‾2‾,‾5‾0‾0

12. 42)‾5‾,‾6‾0‾0   **13.** 4)‾3‾2‾9   **14.** 50)‾5‾,‾4‾3‾2

Module 4: Section B Lesson 6

Name _____

SKILL
WORKSHEET
111

List the common factors of the numbers.
Circle the Greatest Common Factor.

1. 4, 16 _____   **2.** 6, 12 _____

3. 7, 42 _____   **4.** 8, 56 _____

5. 32, 48 _____   **6.** 27, 36 _____

7. 24, 30 _____   **8.** 21, 28 _____

9. 6, 9, 12 _____   **10.** 8, 16, 24 _____

11. 10, 20, 30 _____   **12.** 6, 12, 18 _____

Write the fraction in simplest form.

13. $\frac{8}{18}$ _____   **14.** $\frac{9}{12}$ _____

15. $\frac{16}{20}$ _____   **16.** $\frac{20}{25}$ _____

17. $\frac{42}{48}$ _____   **18.** $\frac{56}{63}$ _____

19. $\frac{40}{72}$ _____   **20.** $\frac{36}{81}$ _____

21. $\frac{24}{32}$ _____   **22.** $\frac{48}{64}$ _____

Module 4: Section B Lesson 7

Name _____

Write the fraction in lowest terms.

1. $\frac{9}{24}$ _____

2. $\frac{9}{18}$ _____

3. $\frac{20}{25}$ _____

4. $\frac{21}{28}$ _____

5. $\frac{10}{28}$ _____

6. $\frac{25}{5}$ _____

7. $\frac{32}{4}$ _____

8. $\frac{22}{33}$ _____

9. $\frac{35}{42}$ _____

10. $\frac{24}{28}$ _____

11. $\frac{32}{48}$ _____

12. $\frac{63}{9}$ _____

13. $\frac{36}{3}$ _____

14. $\frac{10}{15}$ _____

15. $\frac{16}{64}$ _____

16. $\frac{8}{10}$ _____

17. $\frac{8}{12}$ _____

18. $\frac{35}{7}$ _____

19. $\frac{56}{7}$ _____

20. $\frac{45}{63}$ _____

21. $\frac{48}{64}$ _____

22. $\frac{63}{77}$ _____

23. $\frac{144}{12}$ _____

24. $\frac{33}{88}$ _____

25. $\frac{42}{54}$ _____

26. $\frac{100}{10}$ _____

Module 4: Section B Lesson 7

Name _____

Find the least common multiple for each pair of numbers.

1. 3, 4 _____ **2.** 7, 5 _____ **3.** 4, 6 _____

4. 2, 12 _____ **5.** 8, 10 _____ **6.** 11, 3 _____

7. 7, 8 _____ **8.** 4, 9 _____ **9.** 4, 5 _____

10. 4, 8 _____ **11.** 3, 6 _____ **12.** 6, 9 _____

13. 4, 7 _____ **14.** 3, 12 _____ **15.** 6, 10 _____

Find the first two common multiples for each pair of numbers.

16. 16, 20 _____ **17.** 12, 10 _____

18. 3, 5 _____ **19.** 6, 8 _____

20. 24, 18 _____ **21.** 7, 3 _____

22. 4, 7 _____ **23.** 2, 6 _____

24. 8, 5 _____ **25.** 10, 15 _____

Module 4: Section B, Lesson 7

Name _____

Use the chart to find out how many tablespoons are in each.

| 3 tsp = 1 tbsp |
| 4 tbsp = c |

1. 5 tsp _____

2. 6 c _____

3. 2 tsp _____

4. 9 c _____

5. 10 c _____

6. 7 tsp _____

7. 4 tsp _____

8. 12 c _____

Use the chart to find out how many cups are in each.

| 8 oz = 1 cup |

9. 12 oz _____

10. 18 oz _____

11. 23 oz _____

12. 65 oz _____

13. 155 oz _____

14. 78 oz _____

15. 5 oz _____

16. 2 oz _____

17. 28 oz _____

18. 44 oz _____

Module 4: Section B Lesson 7

Name _____

List the first five multiples.

1. 15 _____

2. 7 _____

3. 12 _____

4. 8 _____

5. 6 _____

6. 4 _____

7. 9 _____

8. 11 _____

9. 10 _____

10. 3 _____

11. 5 _____

12. 16 _____

13. 20 _____

14. 14 _____

Module 4: Section C Lesson 8

Name _____

Compare. Use >, <, or =.

1. $\frac{5}{7}$ ◯ $\frac{2}{3}$ 2. $\frac{7}{8}$ ◯ $\frac{4}{5}$ 3. $\frac{5}{9}$ ◯ $\frac{3}{4}$

4. $\frac{3}{5}$ ◯ $\frac{7}{10}$ 5. $\frac{1}{2}$ ◯ $\frac{4}{7}$ 6. $\frac{5}{6}$ ◯ $\frac{7}{9}$

7. $\frac{1}{4}$ ◯ $\frac{2}{5}$ 8. $\frac{2}{9}$ ◯ $\frac{1}{4}$ 9. $\frac{3}{4}$ ◯ $\frac{2}{3}$

10. $\frac{4}{5}$ ◯ $\frac{5}{6}$ 11. $\frac{1}{2}$ ◯ $\frac{1}{3}$ 12. $\frac{2}{3}$ ◯ $\frac{4}{5}$

13. $\frac{1}{4}$ ◯ $\frac{3}{8}$ 14. $\frac{5}{6}$ ◯ $\frac{6}{7}$ 15. $\frac{3}{4}$ ◯ $\frac{7}{8}$

Order the fractions from greatest to least.

16. $\frac{1}{3}, \frac{1}{2}, \frac{1}{4}, \frac{1}{5}$ _____

17. $\frac{2}{3}, \frac{3}{4}, \frac{4}{5}, \frac{7}{8}$ _____

18. $\frac{5}{6}, \frac{9}{10}, \frac{5}{7}, \frac{6}{8}$ _____

19. $\frac{3}{8}, \frac{4}{7}, \frac{7}{10}, \frac{5}{9}$ _____

20. $\frac{3}{7}, \frac{5}{8}, \frac{4}{9}, \frac{7}{10}$ _____

21. Do you use multiples or factors
to compare fractions? _____

Module 4: Section C Lesson 8

Name _____

Write the percents as fractions and the fractions as percents.

1. 97% _____

2. $\frac{22}{100}$ _____

3. $\frac{17}{100}$ _____

4. 42% _____

5. 39% _____

6. $\frac{93}{100}$ _____

7. $\frac{67}{100}$ _____

8. 88% _____

9. 75% _____

10. $\frac{56}{100}$ _____

11. 62% _____

12. $\frac{47}{100}$ _____

13. $\frac{16}{100}$ _____

14. 58% _____

15. 35% _____

16. $\frac{70}{100}$ _____

17. $\frac{29}{100}$ _____

18. 65% _____

19. 12% _____

20. $\frac{30}{100}$ _____

21. $\frac{25}{100}$ _____

22. 79% _____

23. 81% _____

24. $\frac{100}{100}$ _____

Module 4: Section C Lesson 8

Name _____

Solve for *n*.

SKILL
118
WORKSHEET

1. $\frac{3}{5} \times \frac{2}{3} = n$ _____

2. $\frac{7}{8} \times \frac{1}{2} = n$ _____

3. $\frac{1}{6} \times \frac{2}{7} = n$ _____

4. $\frac{4}{5} \times 5 = n$ _____

5. $\frac{1}{4} \times \frac{1}{9} = n$ _____

6. $\frac{2}{3} \times \frac{2}{3} = n$ _____

7. $\frac{5}{7} \times \frac{3}{7} = n$ _____

8. $n \times \frac{5}{6} = \frac{5}{6}$ _____

9. $\frac{3}{5} \times 2 = n$ _____

10. $4 \times \frac{2}{3} = n$ _____

11. $\frac{1}{12} \times \frac{3}{5} = n$ _____

12. $\frac{6}{7} \times \frac{3}{4} = n$ _____

13. $\frac{7}{8} \times n = \frac{7}{8}$ _____

14. $\frac{1}{2} \times \frac{1}{3} = n$ _____

15. $n = \frac{7}{9} \times 1$ _____

16. $n \times \frac{4}{5} = \frac{4}{5}$ _____

17. $\frac{1}{3} \times \frac{1}{3} = n$ _____

18. $\frac{5}{8} \times 6 = n$ _____

19. $8 \times \frac{1}{2} = n$ _____

20. $n = \frac{5}{7} \times \frac{1}{3}$ _____

21. $\frac{7}{10} \times n = \frac{7}{10}$ _____

22. $0 \times \frac{1}{4} = n$ _____

23. $n = 6 \times \frac{1}{3}$ _____

24. $\frac{1}{2} \times \frac{1}{2} = n$ _____

Module 4: Section C Lesson 8

Name _____

Change the improper fractions to mixed numbers.

1. $\frac{7}{4}$ _____

2. $\frac{9}{5}$ _____

3. $\frac{8}{3}$ _____

4. $\frac{13}{8}$ _____

5. $\frac{11}{5}$ _____

6. $\frac{22}{3}$ _____

7. $\frac{13}{7}$ _____

8. $\frac{13}{6}$ _____

9. $\frac{27}{8}$ _____

10. $\frac{23}{4}$ _____

11. $\frac{12}{3}$ _____

12. $\frac{21}{3}$ _____

13. $\frac{46}{7}$ _____

14. $\frac{49}{8}$ _____

15. $\frac{63}{10}$ _____

16. $\frac{31}{5}$ _____

17. $\frac{59}{7}$ _____

18. $\frac{74}{9}$ _____

Change the mixed numbers to fractions.

19. $5\frac{1}{3}$ _____

20. $2\frac{7}{8}$ _____

21. $3\frac{2}{9}$ _____

22. $2\frac{5}{7}$ _____

23. $4\frac{2}{5}$ _____

24. $6\frac{1}{2}$ _____

25. $9\frac{3}{4}$ _____

26. $7\frac{5}{6}$ _____

27. $2\frac{4}{5}$ _____

28. $6\frac{4}{9}$ _____

29. $5\frac{3}{8}$ _____

30. $8\frac{5}{7}$ _____

Module 4: Section C Lesson 9

Name _____

Write the number of feet equivalent to the number of miles.

$$1 \text{ mile} = 5{,}280 \text{ feet}$$
$$1 \text{ yard} = 3 \text{ feet}$$
$$1 \text{ foot} = 12 \text{ inches}$$

1. 4 miles _____

2. $1\frac{1}{2}$ miles _____

3. $\frac{3}{4}$ mile _____

4. 3 miles _____

5. $\frac{1}{4}$ mile _____

6. $\frac{1}{3}$ mile _____

Write the number of yards equivalent to the number of miles.

7. 5 miles _____

8. 10 miles _____

9. $\frac{3}{4}$ mile _____

10. $\frac{1}{2}$ mile _____

Describe each measurement as a fraction of a foot.

11. 2 inches _____

12. 5 inches _____

13. 1 inch _____

14. 9 inches _____

15. 6 inches _____

16. 4 inches _____

Module 4: Section C Lesson 9

Name _____

Read the following problems and solve.

1. Your cat eats 6 ounces of food every day. One can of cat food contains 8 oz.

   a. How many cans of food do you need each week? _____

   b. How long will 4 cans last? _____

   c. How many cans of food do you need every 6 days? _____

2. You are planning a party with 24 guests. You decide to serve hoagies, and estimate that each guest will eat about $\frac{2}{5}$ of a hoagie.

   a. How many hoagies should you buy? _____

   b. Will there be any left over? _____

   c. If so, how much? _____

Name _____

Order these fractions from greatest to least.

1. $\frac{2}{3}, \frac{3}{4}, \frac{4}{5}$ _____

2. $\frac{1}{3}, \frac{5}{6}, \frac{3}{5}$ _____

3. $\frac{1}{2}, \frac{2}{5}, \frac{4}{6}$ _____

4. $\frac{1}{4}, \frac{7}{8}, \frac{3}{7}$ _____

5. $\frac{4}{7}, \frac{5}{6}, \frac{5}{8}$ _____

Change the following fractions greater than one into mixed numbers. Order them from least to greatest.

6. $\frac{20}{4}, \frac{25}{6}, \frac{30}{7}$ _____

7. $\frac{32}{5}, \frac{16}{3}, \frac{21}{4}$ _____

8. $\frac{26}{3}, \frac{66}{8}, \frac{49}{6}$ _____

9. $\frac{14}{4}, \frac{29}{9}, \frac{20}{6}$ _____

10. $\frac{34}{8}, \frac{32}{7}, \frac{9}{2}$ _____

Module 4: Section C Lesson 9

Name _____

Find the sum. Change any fraction greater than one into a mixed number, and write your answers in lowest terms.

1. $\frac{1}{8} + \frac{1}{4} =$ _____

2. $1\frac{1}{2} + 2\frac{1}{5} =$ _____

3. $3\frac{2}{3} + 7\frac{1}{4} =$ _____

4. $\frac{3}{4} + \frac{3}{8} =$ _____

5. $2\frac{1}{3} + 3\frac{1}{2} =$ _____

6. $\frac{5}{6} + \frac{3}{4} =$ _____

7. $1\frac{2}{3} + 8\frac{3}{7} =$ _____

8. $\frac{1}{8} + \frac{1}{2} =$ _____

9. $\frac{3}{10} + \frac{3}{4} =$ _____

10. $2\frac{7}{10} + 1\frac{1}{2} =$ _____

11. $\frac{5}{8} + \frac{1}{2} =$ _____

12. $2\frac{2}{3} + 4\frac{1}{2} =$ _____

Module 4: Section D Lesson 10

Name _____

Decide if the sums will be the same.
Write *yes* if they are. Write *no* if they are not.

1. $3\frac{1}{2} + 2\frac{2}{3} + 4\frac{1}{6}$ _____ $3\frac{4}{8} + 1\frac{5}{3} + 4\frac{2}{12}$

2. $6\frac{3}{4} + 1\frac{1}{3} + 5\frac{1}{4}$ _____ $6\frac{6}{8} + \frac{4}{3} + 5\frac{2}{8}$

3. $7\frac{1}{8} + 2\frac{2}{6} + 3\frac{1}{2}$ _____ $7\frac{2}{4} + 2\frac{1}{3} + \frac{7}{2}$

4. $6\frac{1}{2} + 8\frac{5}{6} + 4\frac{1}{3}$ _____ $6\frac{35}{70} + \frac{53}{6} + 4\frac{12}{36}$

5. $\frac{32}{5} + \frac{70}{10} + 2\frac{7}{8}$ _____ $6\frac{2}{5} + \frac{7}{10} + \frac{25}{8}$

6. $9\frac{1}{4} + 8 + \frac{54}{6}$ _____ $\frac{37}{4} + \frac{96}{12} + 9$

7. $2\frac{1}{5} + 21 + \frac{1}{8}$ _____ $2\frac{5}{20} + \frac{42}{2} + \frac{8}{64}$

8. $6\frac{7}{9} + \frac{81}{9} + 12$ _____ $6\frac{21}{27} + \frac{1}{9} + \frac{144}{12}$

9. $\frac{1}{6} + 2\frac{5}{8} + \frac{59}{7}$ _____ $\frac{36}{6} + 1\frac{13}{8} + 8\frac{1}{7}$

10. $6 + \frac{1}{4} + \frac{2}{4}$ _____ $\frac{72}{12} + \frac{20}{100} + \frac{45}{90}$

11. $2\frac{1}{3} + 3\frac{1}{2} + \frac{4}{5}$ _____ $3\frac{1}{2} + \frac{4}{5} + 2\frac{1}{3}$

12. What property did you use to answer Exercise 11?

_____

Module 4: Section D Lesson 10

Name _____

Find the product. Change any fraction greater than one into a mixed number, and write your answers in lowest terms.

1. $\frac{3}{4} \times 7 =$ _____   2. $\frac{2}{3} \times \frac{3}{5} =$ _____

3. $\frac{1}{5} \times 9 =$ _____   4. $\frac{2}{7} \times \frac{1}{4} =$ _____

5. $2 \times \frac{3}{4} =$ _____   6. $3 \times \frac{7}{8} =$ _____

7. $\frac{1}{2} \times \frac{11}{16} =$ _____   8. $3 \times \frac{3}{8} =$ _____

9. $6 \times \frac{2}{3} =$ _____   10. $\frac{3}{4} \times \frac{1}{16} =$ _____

Find the difference. Change any fraction greater than one into a mixed number, and write your answers in lowest terms.

11. $5\frac{7}{8} - 1\frac{1}{4} =$ _____   12. $2\frac{1}{2} - 1\frac{3}{8} =$ _____

13. $8\frac{3}{4} - 2\frac{1}{8} =$ _____   14. $6\frac{1}{5} - 3\frac{2}{10} =$ _____

15. $15\frac{1}{3} - 7\frac{2}{9} =$ _____   16. $3\frac{3}{4} - 2\frac{3}{8} =$ _____

Module 4: Section D Lesson 11

Name _____

Add only the mixed numbers whose sums are greater than 10.

1. $2\frac{3}{10} + 7\frac{2}{3} =$ _____

2. $5\frac{5}{8} + 4\frac{2}{3} =$ _____

3. $6\frac{2}{3} + 1\frac{3}{16} =$ _____

4. $8\frac{1}{2} + 2\frac{5}{8} =$ _____

5. $2\frac{5}{8} + 7\frac{2}{3} =$ _____

6. $4\frac{5}{12} + 5\frac{2}{3} =$ _____

7. $4\frac{1}{4} + 5\frac{1}{3} =$ _____

8. $9\frac{1}{8} + \frac{10}{12} =$ _____

Find only the differences that are less than four.

9. $8\frac{1}{2} - 5\frac{3}{8} =$ _____

10. $9\frac{3}{4} - 5\frac{1}{2} =$ _____

11. $10 - 5\frac{8}{16} =$ _____

12. $12\frac{2}{3} - 9\frac{1}{4} =$ _____

13. $7 - 3\frac{1}{8} =$ _____

14. $16\frac{2}{3} - 12\frac{1}{2} =$ _____

Module 4: Section D Lesson 11

Name _____

Estimate the quotient.

1. $35\overline{)7,200}$ 2. $15\overline{)3,100}$ 3. $10\overline{)4,900}$

4. $5\overline{)3,040}$ 5. $41\overline{)1,700}$ 6. $30\overline{)9,200}$

7. $19\overline{)8,100}$ 8. $26\overline{)5,300}$ 9. $45\overline{)9,000}$

10. $50\overline{)2,600}$ 11. $69\overline{)5,000}$ 12. $91\overline{)2,800}$

13. $80\overline{)1,700}$ 14. $61\overline{)3,700}$ 15. $100\overline{)1,200}$

16. $39\overline{)2,400}$ 17. $21\overline{)1,600}$ 18. $16\overline{)4,500}$

19. $51\overline{)3,400}$ 20. $43\overline{)4,700}$ 21. $28\overline{)5,900}$

Module 4: Section D Lesson 11

Name _____

SKILL
128
WORKSHEET

For each amount write the fewest pennies, nickels, dimes, quarters, and dollars you would get in change from a $10 bill.

1. $6.43 _____

2. $8.29 _____

3. $7.55 _____

4. $9.15 _____

5. $5.75 _____

6. $7.89 _____

7. $6.72 _____

8. $8.10 _____

9. $9.27 _____

10. $5.36 _____

11. $6.50 _____

12. $7.05 _____

Module 4: Section D Lesson 11

Name _____

Convert the decimal to a fraction.

1. 0.23 = _____   **2.** 0.65 = _____

3. 0.78 = _____   **4.** 0.92 = _____

5. 0.04 = _____   **6.** 0.17 = _____

7. 0.09 = _____   **8.** 0.11 = _____

9. 0.63 = _____   **10.** 0.01 = _____

Write the fraction as a decimal.

11. $\frac{88}{100}$ = _____   **12.** $\frac{37}{100}$ = _____

13. $\frac{96}{100}$ = _____   **14.** $\frac{119}{100}$ = _____

15. $\frac{5}{100}$ = _____   **16.** $\frac{16}{100}$ = _____

17. $\frac{101}{100}$ = _____   **18.** $\frac{67}{100}$ = _____

19. $\frac{10}{100}$ = _____   **20.** $\frac{25}{100}$ = _____

21. $\frac{32}{100}$ = _____   **22.** $\frac{141}{100}$ = _____

Module 5: Section A Lesson 1

Name _____

Write the fraction as a decimal.

1. $\frac{77}{100}$ = _____

2. $\frac{123}{100}$ = _____

3. $\frac{61}{100}$ = _____

4. $\frac{1}{100}$ = _____

5. $\frac{217}{100}$ = _____

6. $\frac{184}{100}$ = _____

7. $\frac{15}{100}$ = _____

8. $\frac{8}{100}$ = _____

9. $\frac{103}{100}$ = _____

10. $\frac{201}{100}$ = _____

11. $\frac{23}{100}$ = _____

12. $\frac{10}{100}$ = _____

13. $\frac{150}{100}$ = _____

14. $\frac{105}{100}$ = _____

Solve.

15. A can is 120 mm high. Write the measurement as a fraction of a meter. Convert the fraction to a decimal.

_____

Module 5: Section A Lesson 1

Name _____

The table below shows the times that some students took to do their homework.

5th Grade Students	Time it takes to do homework
George	1.1 hours
Juanita	0.75 hours
Kim	0.9 hours
Niki	0.35 hours
Jesse	1.19 hours
Steve	0.57 hours
Pablo	1.3 hours
Aimee	1.36 hours
Karen	0.4 hours
Melissa	2.04 hours

1. Order the times of George, Kim, Pablo and Karen from fastest to slowest.

   _____

   _____

2. Order the times of Juanita, Niki, Jesse, Steve, Aimee and Melissa from fastest to slowest.

_____

3. Order the times from fastest to slowest.

_____

_____

Module 5: Section A Lesson 1

Name _____

The table below shows winning times for the men's 100 meter race at the Olympic Games from 1948 to 1984.

Year	Runner	Time
1948	Harrison Dillard, United States	10.3
1952	Lindy Remigino, United States	10.4
1956	Bobby Morrow, United States	10.5
1960	Armin Hary, Germany	10.2
1964	Bob Hayes, United States	10.0
1968	Jim Hines, United States	9.95
1972	Valery Borzov, Soviet Union	10.14
1976	Hasely Crawford, Trinidad	10.06
1980	Allan Wells, Great Britian	10.25
1984	Carl Lewis, United States	9.99

1. Order the times from slowest to fastest.

_____

_____

2. Who has the fastest time? _____

3. Who has the slowest time? _____

Module 5: Section A Lesson 1

Name _____

Use the digits to answer the questions.

5   7   8   6

1. Write the largest number to the
   thousandths' place that has these digits. _____

2. Round the number in
   Exercise 1 to the hundredths' place. _____

3. Round the number in
   Exercise 1 to the tenths' place. _____

4. Round the number in
   Exercise 1 to the ones' place. _____

5. Write the smallest number to the
   thousandths' place that
   has the above digits. _____

6. Round the number in Exercise 5
   to the hundredths' place. _____

7. Round the number in
   Exercise 5 to the tenths' place. _____

Module 5: Section A Lesson 2

Name _____

Round to the nearest tenths' place.

1. 7.14   **2.** 6.92   **3.** 1.88

_____   _____   _____

4. 4.76   **5.** 5.33   **6.** 8.92

_____   _____   _____

Round to the hundredths' place.

7. 4.553   **8.** 1.230   **9.** 6.785

_____   _____   _____

10. 2.376   **11.** 0.006   **12.** 3.985

_____   _____   _____

Module 5: Section A Lesson 2

Name _____

Add.

1. 12.3
+ 3.6

2. 17.7
+ 21.8

3. 11.45
+ 15.44

4. 26.18
+ 12.57

5. 33.737
+ 37.682

6. 26.653
+ 18.887

Subtract.

7. 9.7
− 5.5

8. 5.9
− 3.8

9. 5.7
− 3.4

10. 11.06
− 9.72

11. 16.50
− 6.97

12. 10.16
− 7.58

Module 5: Section A Lesson 2

Name _____

Subtract.

1. 4.8
   – 1.5

2. 7.5
   – 3.1

3. 9.3
   – 6.7

4. 6.85
   – 4.43

5. 9.75
   – 5.44

6. 10.37
   – 7.73

7. 13.12
   – 4.78

8. 9.26
   – 1.98

9. 10.578
   – 8.760

10. 8.966
   – 0.459

11. 6.323
   – 4.237

12. 8.115
   – 7.919

Module 5: Section A Lesson 2

Name _____

Order from smallest to largest.

1. 5 m, 21 cm, 10 km

_____

2. 1 km, 35 cm, 24 m

_____

3. 99 cm, 12 m, 2 km

_____

4. 16 m, 12 cm, 42 km

_____

5. 1,345 kL, 67 mL, 4 L

_____

6. 107 g, 1 kg, 1,178 dg

_____

Rewrite 17 km in the unit indicated.

7. cm _____ **8.** dm _____ **9.** m _____

Module 5: Section B Lesson 3

Name _____

Rewrite 13 grams in the unit indicated.

1. _____ mg

2. _____ cg

3. _____ dg

4. _____ kg

Order from least to greatest.

5. 6.315, 6.19, 6.5, 5.9 _____

6. 0.77, 1.003, 0.749, 1.3 _____

7. $\frac{2}{3}$, $\frac{5}{6}$, $\frac{5}{12}$, $\frac{7}{12}$ _____

8. $1\frac{1}{3}$, $\frac{15}{16}$, $1\frac{5}{12}$, $1\frac{1}{4}$ _____

Round to tenths and order from least to greatest.

9. 8.64 cm, 1.33 cm, 4.67 m, 9.81 m _____

10. 10.21 mm, 0.96 cm, 1.05 dm, 10.05 cm

_____

11. 1.77 mL, 1.34 L, 1.74 mL, 1.55 L _____

12. 7.81 kg, 8.42 kg, 9.83 g, 6.26 g _____

Module 5: Section B Lesson 3

Name _____

Estimate in centimeters.

1. the width of a pencil _____

2. the length of a sheet of paper _____

3. the length of your shoe _____

4. the width of a nickel _____

Measure each object in Exercises 1–4. Find the difference between your estimate and the measurement.

5. the width of a pencil _____

6. the length of a sheet of paper _____

7. the length of your shoe _____

8. the width of a nickel _____

Module 5: Section B Lesson 3

Name _____

Estimate in meters.

1. the length of a bed _____

2. the height of a stove _____

3. the height of a door _____

4. the length of a floor _____

Match the measurement with the object.

5. the length of a table _____   a. 20 kg

6. the capacity of a pot _____   b. 80 L

7. the capacity of an aquarium _____   c. 1.2 m

8. the mass of a dog _____   d. 4 m

9. the mass of a bag of flour _____   e. 2,500 g

10. the length of a car _____   f. 8 L

Module 5: Section B Lesson 3

Name _____

Which metric unit would you use to measure each object?

1. length of a pool _____

2. capacity of a milk carton _____

3. height of a bicycle _____

4. width of a bowl _____

5. distance across a lake _____

6. height of your school _____

7. length of your fingers _____

8. capacity of a drinking fountain _____

9. length of a bathtub _____

10. distance across a field _____

Change to the indicated unit.

11. 1,127 g = _____ kg   **12.** 1.33 L = _____ mL

13. 253 cm = _____ m   **14.** 1,471 cm = _____ km

    Module 5: Section B Lesson 4

Name _____

Which metric unit would you use to measure each object?

1. length of the chalkboard _____

2. capacity of a raindrop _____

3. length of your math book _____

4. height of a telephone pole _____

5. mass of a piece of paper _____

6. width of a television screen _____

7. How would you lift something that is 0.01 km long?

_____

8. How would you move something
that has a mass of 1.5 kg? _____

9. How would you move something that is 12 m
long over a distance of 600 m?

_____

Module 5: Section B Lesson 4

Name _____

Solve.

1. A washing machine has a capacity of
   30 L of water. How many liters of water will it take
   to do 3 loads of wash?

   _____

2. Each person in Rebecca's family drinks 200 mL of
   water for dinner. How many liters of water will she
   serve her family of 6?

   _____

3. A piece of wood has a mass of 750 g. What is the
   mass in kilograms of 8 pieces of wood?

   _____

4. A watering can holds one liter of water. Takeo has
   5 large plants and 3 smaller plants. The large plants
   take about $\frac{1}{2}$ liter, and the small plants about $\frac{1}{4}$
   liter. How many times will Takeo refill the can?

   _____

Module 5: Section B Lesson 4

Name _____

Solve.

1. Mario invites 7 friends for a barbecue.
   Each person eats 250 g of meat.
   How many kilograms of meat should
   he buy?

   _____

2. A hamster eats 50 g of food each day.
   How many kilograms of food will the
   hamster eat in 35 days?

   _____

3. A cement block has a mass of $4\frac{1}{2}$ kg. What is the
   mass in kilograms of 7 blocks?

   _____

4. Tricia is shopping for food for her family for the
   week. Her family drinks 750 mL of juice each day.
   How many 1 L bottles of juice should she buy for
   the week?

   _____

Name _____

Multiply.

SKILL
WORKSHEET
145

1. 0.2
× 5

2. 0.3
× 4

3. 0.8
× 9

4. 0.6
× 7

5. 0.1
× 8

6. 0.3
× 6

7. 0.2
× 9

8. 0.4
× 5

9. 0.8
× 7

10. 1.1
× 3

11. 1.2
× 3

12. 2.2
× 7

Module 5: Section C Lesson 5

Name _____

Multiply.

1. 0.6
    × 2
━━━━

2. 0.3
    × 5
━━━━

3. 0.5
    × 6
━━━━

4. 0.6
    × 9
━━━━

5. 1.5
    × 2
━━━━

6. 1.3
    × 3
━━━━

7. 1.4
    × 6
━━━━

8. 2.3
    × 4
━━━━

9. 2.7
    × 3
━━━━

10. 1.8
    × 7
━━━━

11. 4.6
    × 7
━━━━

12. 5.5
    × 9
━━━━

Module 5: Section C Lesson 5

Name _____

Multiply.

1.   0.5
  × 0.7

2.   0.8
  × 0.2

3.   0.4
  × 0.3

4.   0.1
  × 0.9

5.   0.6
  × 0.5

6.   0.7
  × 0.6

7.   0.3
  × 0.3

8.   0.9
  × 0.2

9.   0.5
  × 0.8

10.   0.3
  × 0.1

11.   0.7
  × 0.2

12.   0.8
  × 0.8

Module 5: Section C Lesson 5

Name _____

Multiply.

1.   0.4
  ×0.9

2.   0.6
  ×0.6

3.   1.3
  ×0.5

4.   1.8
  ×0.4

5.   1.4
  ×1.6

6.   2.1
  ×1.3

7.   2.5
  ×2.6

8.   4.2
  ×2.5

9.   0.36
  × 1.3

10.   0.21
  × 3.4

11.   0.35
  ×0.42

12.   0.17
  ×0.38

Module 5: Section C   Lesson 5

Name _____

SKILL
149
WORKSHEET

Multiply.

1. 1.8
× 0.6

2. 3.5
× 1.4

3. 7.7
× 2.3

4. 6.8
× 4.5

5. 4.7
× 3.4

6. 8.5
× 4.2

Add. Then multiply.

7. 7.3 + 9.2 = _____ × 0.4 = _____

8. 8.1 + 6.0 = _____ × 0.5 = _____

9. 3.2 + 4.8 = _____ × 0.7 = _____

10. 5.6 + 9.3 = _____ × 0.2 = _____

11. 4.0 + 4.7 = _____ × 0.3 = _____

12. 1.8 + 2.6 = _____ × 0.6= _____

Module 5: Section C Lesson 6

Name _____

Multiply.

1.   1.6   **2.**   3.2   **3.**   6.7
   × 0.4   × 0.7   × 3.5

4.   8.3   **5.**   5.3   **6.**   0.45
   × 5.8   × 5.5   × 6.6

Add. Then multiply.

7. $2.3 + 8.1 =$ _____ $\times 0.8 =$ _____

8. $9.4 + 1.5 =$ _____ $\times 0.1 =$ _____

9. $6.5 + 3.4 =$ _____ $\times 0.9 =$ _____

10. $7.6 + 5.2 =$ _____ $\times 0.5 =$ _____

11. $8.2 + 6.9 =$ _____ $\times 0.3 =$ _____

12. $3.4 + 7.7 =$ _____ $\times 0.6 =$ _____

Module 5: Section C Lesson 6

Name _____

Solve.

Sasha and his friends are participating in a variety show at school. The dance they have chosen to perform has a degree of difficulty of 3.2. The judges' marks for their dance are as follows.

8.5   7.8   9.0   8.0   9.5   9.6   9.0

1. The highest and lowest scores are dropped. Which scores should be dropped? _____

2. Add the remaining marks. What is the sum for their dance? _____

3. Multiply the sum by the degree of difficulty, 3.2. What is the product? _____

4. Multiply the product in Exercise 3 by 0.6. What was his team's final score? _____

5. Write a number sentence that shows how to find their score from the five marks.

_____

Module 5: Section C Lesson 6

Name _____

Solve.

Tanya performs in a diving competition. The judges' marks for her dive are as follows.

9.50   9.75   9.60   9.80   9.60   9.25   9.50

1. The highest and lowest marks are dropped. Which marks should be dropped? _____

2. Add the remaining marks. _____

3. Multiply the sum in Exercise 2 by the degree of difficulty, 3.8. _____

4. Multiply the product in Exercise 3 by 0.6. What is her score? _____

5. Write a number sentence that shows how to find her score from the five marks.

_____

Module 5: Section C Lesson 6

Name _____

Find the average.

1. 1.2, 1.3, 2.3 _____

2. 7.8, 5.5, 5.9 _____

3. 3.2, 4.3, 5.7 _____

4. 4.1, 6.8, 1.1 _____

5. 9.1, 3.8, 7.5 _____

6. 1.35, 1.75, 3.50 _____

Solve.

7. The cheerleading team scored 5.1, 5.3, and 5.2 in the county finals. What was the cheerleading team's average score?

_____

8. Nikita received the following scores in a singing contest: 3.3, 3.0, and 2.7. What was Nikita's average score?

_____

Module 5: Section D Lesson 7

Name _____

Find the average.

1. 1.7, 2.4, 1.6 _____

2. 8.3, 6.5, 5.9 _____

3. 6.4, 9.8, 5.4 _____

4. 7.7, 4.8, 10.3 _____

5. 9.75, 9.25, 9.80 _____

6. 13.55, 23.68, 17.07 _____

Solve.

7. Elias performs in an ice-dancing contest. The judges give him the marks 9.6, 8.8, and 9.2. What is his average score?

_____

8. Tina's puppy Sparky scored 9.9, 9.8, and 9.4 in the dog show. What was his average score?

_____

Module 5: Section D Lesson 7

Name _____

Divide.

1. $6\overline{)42.6}$

2. $3\overline{)67.2}$

3. $5\overline{)89.5}$

4. $8\overline{)95.2}$

5. $6\overline{)94.2}$

6. $8\overline{)65.25}$

Module 5: Section D Lesson 7

Name _____

Divide.

1. 5⟌38.5

2. 3⟌78.9

3. 7⟌93.8

4. 6⟌77.4

5. 9⟌12.42

6. 6⟌4.74

Name _____

Change each decimal to a fraction in lowest terms.

SKILL
157
WORKSHEET

1. $0.2 =$ _____

2. $0.242 =$ _____

3. $0.46 =$ _____

4. $0.675 =$ _____

5. $0.568 =$ _____

6. $0.27 =$ _____

7. $0.010 =$ _____

8. $0.333 =$ _____

9. $0.945 =$ _____

10. $0.156 =$ _____

11. $0.875 =$ _____

12. $0.64 =$ _____

Module 5: Section D Lesson 8

Name _____

Change each decimal to a fraction in lowest terms.

SKILL
158
WORKSHEET

1. $0.12 =$ _____

2. $0.05 =$ _____

3. $0.389 =$ _____

4. $0.003 =$ _____

5. $0.148 =$ _____

6. $0.444 =$ _____

7. $0.009 =$ _____

8. $0.013 =$ _____

9. $0.123 =$ _____

10. $0.40 =$ _____

11. $0.625 =$ _____

12. $0.72 =$ _____

Module 5: Section D Lesson 8

Name _____

Change each fraction to a decimal.
Round to the thousandths' place.

1. $\frac{1}{4}$ = _____   2. $\frac{1}{5}$ = _____

3. $\frac{1}{6}$ = _____   4. $\frac{2}{9}$ = _____

5. $\frac{5}{8}$ = _____   6. $\frac{6}{7}$ = _____

7. $\frac{7}{9}$ = _____   8. $\frac{2}{3}$ = _____

9. $\frac{4}{5}$ = _____   10. $\frac{3}{4}$ = _____

Module 5: Section D Lesson 8

Name _____

Change each fraction to a decimal.
Round to the thousandths' place.

1. $\frac{4}{9}$ = _____   2. $\frac{7}{8}$ = _____

3. $\frac{7}{10}$ = _____   4. $\frac{8}{20}$ = _____

5. $\frac{3}{11}$ = _____   6. $\frac{6}{10}$ = _____

7. $\frac{3}{20}$ = _____   8. $\frac{5}{9}$ = _____

9. $\frac{9}{10}$ = _____   10. $\frac{6}{20}$ = _____

Module 5: Section D Lesson 8

Name _____

Record the latitude and longitude for
the points shown on the map.

1. _____

2. _____

3. _____

4. _____

5. _____

6. _____

7. _____

8. _____

9. _____

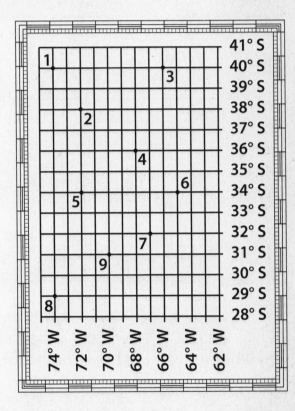

Module 6: Section A Lesson 1

Name _____

Plot the following locations on the grid, and label them 1–6.

1. 11° S, 37° W   **2.** 16° S, 32° W   **3.** 14° S, 35° W

4. 12° S, 32° W   **5.** 17° S, 36° W   **6.** 15° S, 37° W

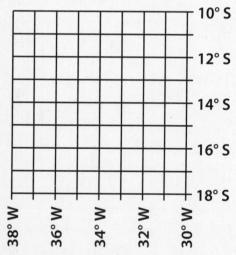

Tell whether you are traveling north, south, east, or west as you move from 14° S, 34° W.

7. 14° S, 32° W _____   **8.** 18° S, 34° W _____

9. 10° S, 34° W _____   **10.** 14° S, 38° W _____

Module 6: Section A Lesson 1

Name _____

Name the figures in the drawing.

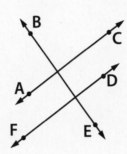

1. Line segments _____

2. Parallel line segments _____

3. Perpendicular line segments _____

4. Write a definition of a ray.
   Name a ray in the drawing. _____

5. Write a definition of a vertex. Name a vertex in
   the drawing.

   _____

Module 6: Section A Lesson 2

Name _____

Draw a shape that is congruent to each shape on the geoboard.

1.

2.

3.

4.

5.

6.

Module 6: Section A Lesson 2

Name _____

Start at (0, 0) on a coordinate grid. Draw an arrow to show the direction an object moves to get to each point.

1. (6, 0) _____   **2.** (0, 5) _____

3. (3, 5) _____   **4.** (5, 0) _____

5. (1, 9) _____   **6.** (8, 9) _____

7. (3, 0) _____   **8.** (3, 6) _____

9. (3, 1) _____   **10.** (7, 1) _____

Tell if you are traveling right, left, up, or down on the grid as you move between the points in each of these pairs.

11. (3, 2) to (3, 8) _____   **12.** (3, 2) to (8, 2) _____

13. (4, 8) to (4, 10) _____   **14.** (4, 10) to (4, 6) _____

15. (4, 6) to (1, 6) _____   **16.** (1, 6) to (1, 9) _____

17. (1, 9) to (3, 9) _____   **18.** (3, 9) to (3, 7) _____

Module 6: Section A Lesson 3

Name _____

Plot and connect each set of points on the grid.

1. (5, 4), (0, 4), (0, 1), (5, 1)

2. (8, 4), (8, 7), (10, 4), (10, 7)

3. (6, 7), (7, 7), (7, 9), (6, 9)

4. (4, 5), (1, 5), (1, 7), (4, 7)

5. Which rectangle is smallest? _____

6. Draw a rectangle that is congruent to the largest rectangle you made.

Name _____

Plot and connect each set of points on the grid.

1. (1, 1), (3, 1), (2, 2)

2. (7, 10), (9, 10), (8, 7)

3. (1, 4), (7, 4), (4, 7)

4. (7, 1), (10, 1), (10, 4)

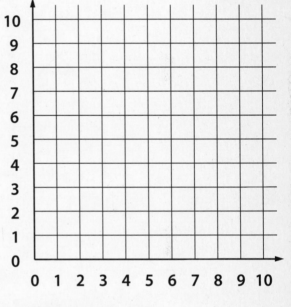

5. Which triangle is a right triangle? _____

6. Double each coordinate from Exercise 1. Draw the new shape on the grid. How does it compare to triangle 1?

_____

Module 6: Section A Lesson 3

Name _____

Write the ordered pairs that make this figure. Start at the ordered pair (1, 1).

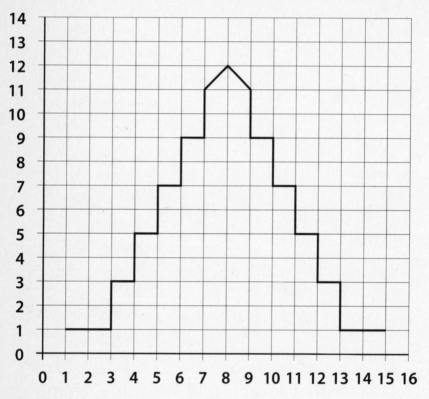

1. _____

_____

Module 6: Section A Lesson 3

Name _____

This is a scale drawing of a desk top.
Measure the length and width of the
drawing. Record those numbers and the
real measurements in the table. Then
figure out the scale.

desktop

3 cm (height) — 4 cm (width)

	Drawing	Real Measurements	Scale
Length	1.	56 cm	5.
Width	2. 3 cm	40 cm	
Diagonal	3.	4.	

Name _____

Use the figure to answer the questions.

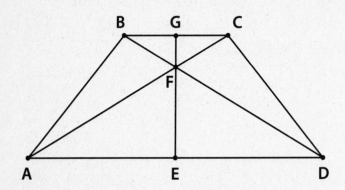

1. What is the vertex of ∠BCD? _____

2. Find an angle that is congruent to ∠AFB. _____

3. Name 4 right angles in the figure.

_____

4. Find a line segment that
is perpendicular to $\overline{AD}$. _____

5. Find two line segments
that are parallel. _____

Name _____

Use your protractor to identify each
angle as *acute, right,* or *obtuse.*

1.

_____

2.
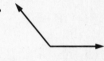

_____

3.

_____

4.

_____

5. On a separate piece of paper use a protractor to
draw angles with the following measures: 85°,
100°, 75°, 140°. Next to each drawing, write
whether the angle is *acute, right,* or *obtuse.*

6. At what times would the hands of a clock show:

  a. a right angle? ____   **b.** a 60° angle? _____

  c. a 30° angle? ____   **d.** a 180° angle? _____

Module 6: Section B Lesson 4

Name _____

Plot each set of ordered pairs on the coordinate grid. Connect the points to form an angle, with its vertex at the second point listed.

1. (1, 1), (3, 1), (3, 3)

2. (1, 7), (4, 7), (4, 10)

3. (6, 4), (6, 1), (9, 1)

4. (8, 5), (10, 7), (8, 9)

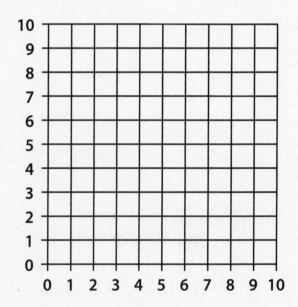

5. How many degrees are in a circle? _____

6. How many 60° angles connected at the vertex with a common side would make a circle? _____

Module 6: Section B Lesson 4

Name _____

Use a ruler to help you name each kind of triangle.

1.
A ◺ B
C

_____

2.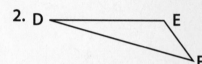
D ◣ E
F

_____

3.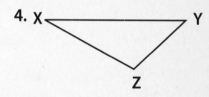
M ◹ N
O

_____

4. X ◺ Y
Z

_____

5. What is the measure of ∠ABC? _____

6. If ∠DEF = 127° and ∠EDF = 15°,
   what is the measure of ∠EFD? _____

7. Angles NMO and NOM are congruent. If
   ∠NMO = 25°, what is the measure of ∠MNO?

_____

Module 6: Section B Lesson 5

Name _____

Measure the following angles:

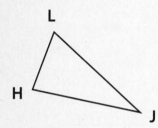

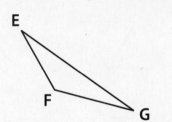

1. ∠EFG _____ **2.** ∠FGE _____

3. ∠FEG _____ **4.** ∠HLJ _____

5. ∠JHL _____ **6.** ∠LJH _____

7. Draw an angle congruent to ∠EFG.

8. Draw an angle congruent to ∠LHJ.

Name _____

Use the triangles to answer the questions.

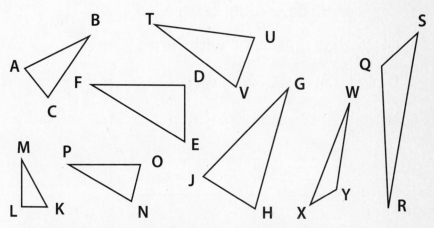

1. Which pairs of triangles are similar?

_____

2. Name an obtuse angle in △QRS. _____

3. Name an angle congruent to ∠RQS. _____

4. What kind of angle is ∠EDF? _____

5. Name two acute angles in △DEF. _____

Module 6: Section B Lesson 5

Name _____

Use your ruler, protractor, and the space at the bottom of the page for drawings.

1. Draw a line 6 cm long. Label it $\overline{AB}$.

2. Draw angle $BAC = 50°$ with vertex A.

3. Draw $\angle CBA = 50°$ with vertex B.

4. Label point C. Measure $\angle ACB$. _____

5. Measure $\overline{CB}$. _____

6. Measure $\overline{CA}$. _____

7. What kind of triangle is $\triangle ABC$? _____

8. Draw another triangle similar to $\triangle ABC$. Label it $\triangle DEF$.

Module 6: Section B Lesson 5

Name _____

Find the lengths of a similar triangle using these ratios.

	Ratio	Sides of a Triangle	Sides of a Similar Triangle
1.	$\frac{1}{4}$	3, 4, 5	
2.	$\frac{2}{1}$	12, 24, 32	
3.	$\frac{1}{10}$	4, 5, 9	
4.	$\frac{7}{1}$	21, 28, 35	
5.	$\frac{1}{100}$	6, 12, 16	
6.	$\frac{5}{1}$	90, 180, 240	

On a separate piece of paper, use the angle measures to draw two similar triangles that show the given ratio.

	Ratio	Angle Measure
7.	$\frac{3}{1}$	40°, 50°, 90°
8.	$\frac{1}{2}$	60°, 60°, 60°

Module 6: Section C Lesson 6

Name _____

Draw a similar triangle for each triangle that is shown. Use the given ratio.

1. Ratio $\frac{2}{1}$

2. Ratio $\frac{1}{4}$

3. Ratio $\frac{2}{1}$

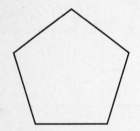

Module 6: Section C Lesson 6

Name _____

Use the larger grid to draw a larger house.

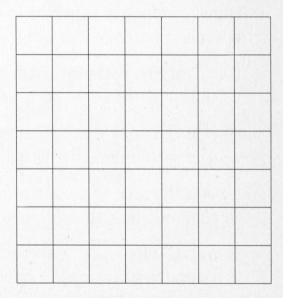

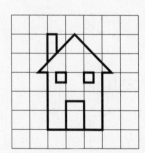

1. What is the ratio between the two houses? _____

2. Estimate the area of the small house if each square is a square centimeter. _____

3. Estimate the area of the large house. _____

4. What is the ratio of the areas? _____

Module 6: Section C Lesson 6

Name _____

Use a ruler, a protractor, and centimeter grid paper to answer the questions.

1. Draw a rectangle 3 cm by 5 cm.
   What is the area of you rectangle? _____

2. Draw another rectangle 6 cm by 10 cm.
   What is the area of the second rectangle? _____

3. What is the ratio of the sides of the smaller rectangle to the larger rectangle? _____

4. What is the ratio of the areas of the smaller rectangle to the larger rectangle? _____

5. Draw any two similar triangles.
   Measure their sides. What is the ratio? _____

6. Estimate the area of each triangle.
   What is the ratio of the areas? _____

Module 6: Section C Lesson 6

Name _____

In the shape below, find the polygons described in the exercises.

1. How many triangles can you find? _____

2. List the triangles.

_____

_____

_____

_____

A   E   B

G   H

D   F   C

3. How many quadrilaterals can you find? _____

4. List the quadrilaterals. _____

_____

5. How many pentagons can you find? _____

Name all the quadrilaterals with:

6. all right angles _____

7. 4 equal sides _____

Module 6: Section C Lesson 7

Name _____

Name each shape.

1.

_____

2.

_____

3.

_____

4.

_____

Write *true* or *false* next to each statement.

5. A rhombus always has 4 equal angles. _____

6. A trapezoid always has 2 parallel sides. _____

7. A rectangle always has 4 right angles. _____

8. A parallelogram always has 2 right angles. _____

Module 6: Section C Lesson 7

Name _____

Use your protractor to measure the angles in each polygon. Label the polygon and write the sum of the angles.

SKILL 183 WORKSHEET

1.

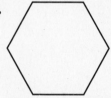

name _____

measure of angle ____

sum of angles _____

2.

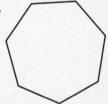

name _____

measure of angle ____

sum of angles _____

3.

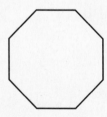

name _____

measure of angle ____

sum of angles _____

4.

name _____

measure of angle ____

sum of angles _____

Module 6: Section C Lesson 7

Name _____

Draw each polygon. Write as many names as you can for each one, give characteristics.

1. rectangle

2. parallelogram

_____

_____

_____

_____

_____

_____

3. trapezoid

4. rhombus

_____

_____

_____

_____

_____

_____

Module 6: Section C Lesson 7

Name _____

How many minutes does it take to walk to school? Here is what 12 fifth graders said.

5, 9, 10, 10, 20, 16, 5, 8, 15, 9, 15, 10

Make or find the following:

1. ordered list _____

2. tally sheet _____

3. line plot _____

4. describe cluster _____

5. longest time _____

6. shortest time _____

7. range _____

8. mean _____

9. median _____

10. mode _____

Module 6: Section D Lesson 8

Name _____

This line plot shows the number of hours of television each student watches each week. Use the line plot to complete the exercises.

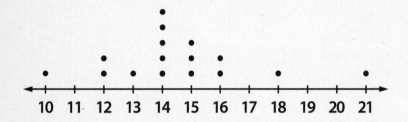

1. What is the least number of hours watched per week? _____

2. What is the greatest number of hours watched per week. _____

3. What is the range? _____

4. What is the mode? _____

5. What is the mean? _____

6. What is the median? _____

Module 6: Section D Lesson 8

Name _____

In 8 games, a basketball player scores the following number of points:

8, 12, 22, 12, 8, 10, 17, 9

1. Make a line plot for scores.

2. What is the median number
of points scored? _____

3. What is the mean number
of points scored? _____

4. What is the mode? _____

5. What is the range ? _____

Module 6: Section D Lesson 8

Name _____

Answer the questions below.

1. Write 5 numbers with a mean of 10.

_____

2. What is the mode? _____

3. What is the range? _____

4. Write 6 numbers with a range of 15.

_____

5. What is the mean? _____

6. What is the median? _____

7. Add one number larger to your list for number 4. Find the new mean. _____

8. Add one number smaller to your list for number 4. Find the new mean. _____

Name _____

This stem-and-leaf plot shows the number of minutes each student reads outside of school each day. Use it to complete the exercises.

0	
1	0, 5
2	0, 0, 0, 5
3	0, 0, 0, 0, 0, 0, 5, 5
4	0, 5, 5, 5, 5
5	0
6	0, 0

How many totals are greater than the following?

1. 20 _____   **2.** 50 _____   **3.** 35 _____

4. 60 _____   **5.** 15 _____   **6.** 45 _____

How many students had these totals?

7. 60 minutes _____   **8.** 30 minutes _____

9. 15 minutes _____   **10.** 20 minutes _____

Module 6: Section D Lesson 9

Name _____

Complete the exercises below.

1. Make a stem-and-leaf plot for the following test scores.

   60, 63, 70, 75, 80, 70, 75, 90, 93, 85

2. What is the mean? _____

3. What is the mode? _____

4. What is the median? _____

5. What is the range? _____

Name _____

Here's a stem-and-leaf plot that shows the number of seconds some students thought they could hold their breath.

0	5, 5, 8, 9, 9
1	0, 0, 0, 5, 5, 5, 5, 9
2	0, 0, 0, 0
3	0
4	
5	0
6	0, 0

Find the following.

1. best middle _____   **2.** biggest cluster ____

3. biggest gap _____   **4.** highest total _____

5. lowest total _____   **6.** range _____

7. a conclusion you can draw from this data

_____

_____

Module 6: Section D Lesson 10

Name _____

Complete the exercises below.

1. Make a stem-and-leaf plot for this data on the number of books some students read in a year:

   20, 25, 10, 5, 30, 26, 28, 35, 48, 23, 42, 43, 26, 27, 3, 15, 20, 18, 25, 30

2. The best middle is _____.

3. The range is _____.

4. What are some conclusions you can draw from this data?

   _____

   _____

Module 6: Section D Lesson 10   © Houghton Mifflin Company. All rights reserved/5

Name _____

Estimate. Then find the circumference for the given diameter.

1.

d = 12 in.

_____

2.

d = 6 in.

_____

3.

d = 8.5 in.

_____

4.

d = 15 in.

_____

Estimate the diameter for the given circumference.

5.

C = 42 in.

_____

6.

C = 23 in.

_____

Module 7: Section A Lesson 1

Name _____

Find the circumference for the circles.

1.

d = 21 ft

_____

2.

d = 5 in.

_____

3.

d = 17 in.

_____

4.

d = 6 in.

_____

5.

d = 14 ft

_____

6.

d = 20 ft

_____

Module 7: Section A Lesson 1

Name _____

Record the diameters and circumference.
Round your answers to the nearest tenth.

1.

r = 4 in.

d = ____   C = ____

2.

r = 10 ft

d = ____   C = ____

3.

r = 3 ft

d = ____   C = ____

4.

r = 8 ft

d = ____   C = ____

5.

r = 11 in.

d = ____   C = ____

6.

r = 12 in.

d = ____   C = ____

Module 7: Section A Lesson 1

Name _____

Use the figures to answer questions 1-5.

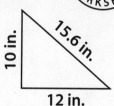

9 in.

9 in.

Figure A

10 in.

8 in.

Figure B

10 in.   15.6 in.

12 in.

Figure C

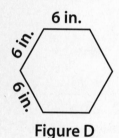

6 in.

6 in.

6 in.

Figure D

12 in.   12 in.

12 in.

Figure E

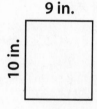

9 in.

10 in.

Figure F

1. Which figures have the same perimeter? _____

2. Which figures have a perimeter greater than 36 in.?

_____

3. Which have sides of equal length? _____

4. Which figure has the larger area, A or B? _____

Module 7: Section A Lesson 1

Name _____

Use the spinner to answer questions 1-3.

1. Write the sample space.

   _____

2. Is the probability of spinning each number
   equally likely? Why or why not?

   _____

   _____

3. Name the probability of spinning each number.

   a. _____   b. _____   c. _____   d. _____

   e. _____   f. _____   g. _____   h. _____

Module 7: Section A Lesson 2

Name _____

Use the spinner to answer questions 1-4.

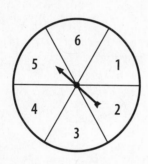

1. What is the probability of
spinning an even number? _____

2. What is the probability of
spinning an odd number? _____

3. What is the probability of
spinning a number less than 4? _____

4. What is the probability of
spinning a number less than 6? _____

Module 7: Section A Lesson 2

Name _____

Use the spinner to answer questions 1-5.

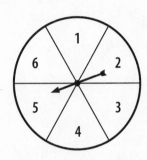

1. What is the probability of
   spinning an even number? _____

2. What other fraction would
   describe the identical outcome? _____

3. What is the probability of
   spinning the number 2? _____

4. What are some other ways
   of expressing the same outcome? _____

5. What is the sample space
   for the spinner? _____

Module 7: Section A Lesson 2

Name _____

Use the spinner to answer questions 1-5.

1. What is the probability of
   spinning an even number? _____

2. What other fraction would
   describe the identical outcome? _____

3. What is the probability of
   spinning the number 7? _____

4. Is there any other fraction which would
   express this outcome? If so, what? _____

5. What is the sample space
   for the spinner? _____

Name _____

SKILL
201
WORKSHEET

A number cube has the numbers 1-6.
Answer questions 1-5.

1. What is the probability of rolling a 1? _____

2. What is the probability of
rolling an even number? _____

3. What other fractions would express the
probability of rolling an even number?

_____

4. What is the sample space for the cube?

_____

5. Express the probability for rolling an odd
number as a fraction and as a decimal.

_____

Module 7: Section B Lesson 3

Name _____

Use the spinner to answer questions 1-5.

1. What is the probability of
   each outcome? How do you know? _____

2. What is the probability of
   spinning a bird? _____

3. Name an event on the
   spinner that has a probability of $\frac{1}{2}$. _____

4. What is the sample space for the spinner?

   _____

5. What is the probability of spinning
   something that sheds? _____

Module 7: Section B Lesson 3

Name _____

Use the spinner to answer questions 1-3.

1. Write the sample space.

_____

_____

_____

_____

2. What is the probability of spinning each number on the spinner? _____

3. Draw a circle graph to display the probability of spinning any even number on the spinner.

Module 7: Section B Lesson 3

Name _____

Use the spinner to answer questions 1-4.

1. Write the sample space.

_____

_____

_____

_____

2. What is the probability of
spinning a number divisible by 5? _____

3. Express this outcome as a fraction,
a decimal, and a percent. _____

_____

4. Draw a circle graph to display the probability of
spinning a number divisible by 4.

Module 7: Section B Lesson 3   © Houghton Mifflin Company. All rights reserved/5

Name _____

A number cube has the numbers 1-6.
Answer questions 1-5.

1. Write the sample space.

   _____

2. What is the probability that
   any one side will be thrown?
   Express as a fraction. _____

3. What is the probability of rolling an even
   number? Express as a fraction, a decimal, and
   a percent.

   _____

4. What is the probability of rolling a 6? _____

5. What other fraction would express the probability
   of rolling a 6?

   _____

Module 7: Section B Lesson 4

Name _____

There are 2 white, 5 green, and 3 yellow
 marbles in a bag. Express the probability
ratio for drawing each color in each of
the following forms.

1. as a fraction _____

2. as a decimal _____

3. as a percent _____

4. in words _____

_____

5. How do you change the way a probability is
   written from a decimal to a percent?

_____

Name _____

Here is a box with 25 white, 25 black, and 50 green ping pong balls. Express the probability ratio for drawing each color in each of the following forms.

Ping Pong
Balls

1. as a fraction _____

2. as a decimal _____

3. as a percent _____

4. in words _____

_____

Module 7: Section B Lesson 4

Name _____

There are 1 red, 2 green, and 7 yellow marbles in a bag. Express the probability ratio for each color as a fraction, as a decimal, and as a percent.

Marbles	Fraction	Decimal	Percent
Red	1.	2.	3.
Green	4	5.	6.
Yellow	7.	8.	9.

Module 7: Section B Lesson 4

Name _____

Use the spinners to answer questions 1-5.

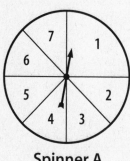

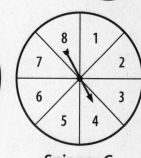

Spinner A   **Spinner B**   **Spinner C**

1. On which spinners are an odd and
   an even number equally probable? _____

2. On which spinner is an even
   number least likely? _____

3. On which spinner is a 1 the
   most likely outcome? _____

4. On which spinner is an odd
   number most likely? _____

5. Which numbers have
   a probability of 0.25? _____

Module 7: Section C Lesson 5

Name _____

Use the spinner to answer questions 1-5.

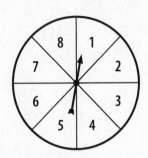

1. What is the probability of spinning a 7? _____

2. What is the probability of spinning
an odd number that is not a 1? _____

3. What is the probability of spinning
a 1 or 2 on the spinner? _____

4. What is the probability of spinning
an even number on the spinner? _____

5. What is the probability of
spinning a 1, 2, or 3? _____

Module 7: Section C Lesson 5   © Houghton Mifflin Company. All rights reserved/5

Name _____

You have entered a drawing to win a new bike. Your ticket has the numbers 2, 1, 7, and 4. The person in charge of the drawing is using 6 numbered ping pong balls to draw the winning number.

1. What is the probability that any one of your numbers will be drawn? _____

2. Write the sample space.

_____

3. What is the probability for drawing an even number? _____

Module 7: Section C Lesson 5

Name _____

Write the probability.

1. Spin a 5 on a spinner with eight equal sections numbered 1-8. _____

2. Roll 3 or 6 on a 1-6 number cube. _____

3. Spin an even number on a spinner that has twelve equal sections numbered 1-12. _____

4. Spin an odd number on a spinner that has 10 equal sections numbered 1-10. _____

5. Spin a 1 on a spinner with four equal sections numbered 1-4. _____

Module 7: Section C Lesson 5

Name _____

Make a tree diagram to show all the possible outcomes of a spinner with equal red, blue, green, and white parts and a 1-6 number cube. Use the diagram to state each probability.

1. red and any even number _____

2. white and 5 _____

3. blue and an odd number _____

4. blue or white and 2 or 4 _____

5. red or blue and any even number _____

Name _____

Make a tree diagram to show all the possible outcomes from flipping a coin and a spinner with 1, 2, and 3 equal parts. Use the diagram to state each probability.

1. heads and 2 _____

2. tails and 1 _____

3. heads and 3 _____

4. tails and any odd number _____

5. heads and 1 or 3 _____

6. heads and an even number _____

Name _____

State each probability without drawing a tree diagram.

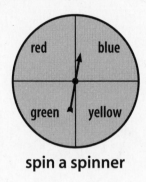

red   blue

green   yellow

spin a spinner

flip a coin

1. blue and tails _____

2. heads and green _____

3. red or green and tails _____

4. heads and blue or red _____

5. tails and any color _____

Module 7: Section C Lesson 6

Name _____

You spin the two spinners shown below. State each probability without drawing a tree diagram.

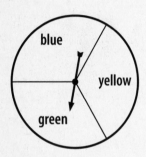
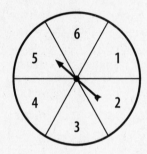

1. blue and any even number _____

2. green or yellow and 3 _____

3. yellow and 1 or 4 _____

4. blue or green and 2 or 5 _____

5. yellow and any odd number _____

Module 7: Section C Lesson 6

Name _____

Look at the spinners. Then answer the questions.

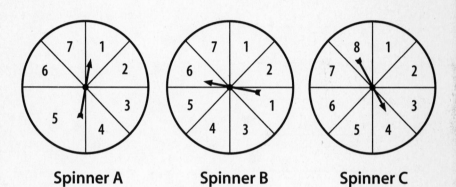

Spinner A   **Spinner B**   **Spinner C**

1. Is spinner A fair? Why or why not?

_____

2. Is spinner B fair? Why or why not?

_____

3. Is spinner C fair? Why or why not?

_____

Module 7: Section D Lesson 7

Name _____

Write the fractions that are equal to $\frac{1}{4}$, $\frac{1}{2}$, $\frac{3}{4}$ or as a percent. Write the fractions that are less than $\frac{1}{2}$ as a decimal.

1. $\frac{2}{8}$ _____

2. $\frac{1}{4}$ _____

3. $\frac{10}{20}$ _____

4. $\frac{15}{50}$ _____

5. $\frac{75}{100}$ _____

6. $\frac{3}{4}$ _____

7. $\frac{4}{5}$ _____

8. $\frac{3}{3}$ _____

9. $\frac{3}{20}$ _____

10. $\frac{20}{25}$ _____

11. $\frac{8}{32}$ _____

12. $\frac{6}{10}$ _____

Module 7: Section D Lesson 7

Name _____

Read the paragraph below. Then answer the questions.

You and another student have challenged each other to a new version of Math Roll. You get a blue number cube, and your partner gets a red number cube. In the game, you multiply the number rolled by 4, then subtract 3 from the product. You score a point if the answer is an even number. Your partner scores a point if the answer is an odd number.

1. What is the probability that you will roll a 5 on the blue number cube? _____

2. What is the probability that your partner will roll a 5 on the red number cube? _____

3. So far, would you say the game is fair or not fair? _____

4. Now, consider the math rules that you must follow. Is the game fair? Why or why not?

_____

Module 7: Section D Lesson 7

Name _____

Read the paragraph below. Then answer the questions.

In Math Roll, the rules have been changed. You play with a yellow number cube and your partner plays with a blue number cube. Multiply the number rolled by 5. Subtract 2 from the product. Then add 1. You score a point if the answer is an even number. Your partner scores a point if the answer is an odd number.

1. Do both players have the same chance to roll the number 4? _____

2. Does the color of the number cube have anything to do with the fairness of the game? _____

3. Is the game fair? Why or why not?

   _____

4. In order to keep Math Roll fair, the multiplier must always be what kind of number? Odd or even?

   _____

Module 7: Section D Lesson 7

Name _____

You roll two number cubes, each numbered 1-6. Write the probability of the roll.

1. two 2's _____

2. a "double" _____

3. a 1 and a 6 _____

4. sum of an odd number _____

5. two even numbers _____

6. a 3 and a 4 _____

7. two 5's _____

8. two odd numbers _____

Module 7: Section D Lesson 8

Name _____

Use the spinners to answer questions
1-6. Write the probability of the spin.

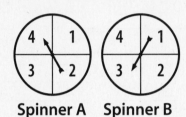

Spinner A   Spinner B

1. two even numbers _____

2. an odd and an even number _____

3. two 4's _____

4. a 3 and a 4 _____

5. doubles _____

6. a 1 and a 3 _____

Module 7: Section D Lesson 8

Name _____

You pick two cards, one from each set numbered 1-4. Write the probability of the pick.

1. two 3's _____

2. an even and an odd number _____

3. sum of the numbers is odd _____

4. two even numbers _____

5. a 2 and a 4 _____

6. Make a tree diagram to show all the possible outcomes.

Module 7: Section D Lesson 8

Name _____

You flip two coins. Write the probability of the flip for questions 1-3.

1. heads _____

2. tails _____

3. heads and tails _____

4. Write the sample space. _____

5. Make a tree diagram to show all the possible outcomes.

Module 7: Section D Lesson 8

Name _____

Fill in the blanks.

1. A _____ can be measured in
   two dimensions: length and width.

2. Space figures (three-dimensional
   objects) have the added dimension of _____.

3. Polygons make up the _____ of space figures.

4. A space figure with all square faces is a _____.

5. What kinds of shapes are these?

a.

_____

b.

_____

c.

_____

d.

_____

e.

_____

f.

_____

Module 8: Section A Lesson 1

Name _____

Identify the number of faces and
vertexes of the following objects.

1. Faces _____

2. Faces _____

3. Vertexes _____

4. Vertexes _____

5. Faces _____

6. Faces _____

7. Vertexes _____

8. Vertexes _____

Module 8: Section A Lesson 1

Name _____

Complete the exercises below.

1. What is a net?

_____

_____

2. From the nets pictured, identify the shapes.

a.

_____

b.

_____

c.

_____

d.

_____

e.

_____

f.

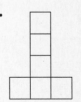

_____

Module 8: Section A Lesson 1

Name _____

Draw nets for the following shapes.

1. rectangular prism

2. cube

3. cylinder

Name _____

How many faces make up the following space figures?

1.

_____

2.

_____

3.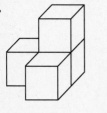

_____

4.

_____

5.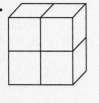

_____

6.

_____

Module 8: Section A Lesson 2

Name _____

How many cubic units are contained in the following space figures?

1.

_____

2.

_____

3.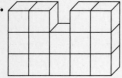

_____

4.

_____

5.

_____

6.

_____

Module 8: Section A Lesson 2

Name _____

Write down the number of faces and the number of cubic units for each space figure below.

Figure A

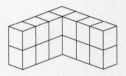

Figure B

1. Faces _____

2. Cubic Units _____

3. Faces _____

4. Cubic Units _____

5. Which figure above has the greatest number of edges? _____

6. How many flat surfaces are contained in Figure C?

_____

Figure C

Module 8: Section A Lesson 2

Name _____

Color all the outside faces of Figure F
and Figure G.

Figure F

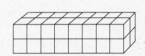

Figure G

1. How many colored faces
   does Figure F have? _____

2. How many colored faces
   does Figure G have? _____

3. How many cubic units
   does Figure F contain? _____

4. If you rearranged the cubes of Figure F to make a
   space figure that looks like
   Figure G, would the
   number of cubes change? _____

Module 8: Section A Lesson 2

Name _____

Answer the following questions.

1. What is the definition of volume?

   _____

2. In what unit of measurement is
   volume usually measured? _____

3. What is a cubic centimeter? _____

4. Find the height of each figure.
   (Assume each edge measures 1 cm.) _____

Figure A   **Figure B**

5. Find the area of the base for each figure.

   Figure A _____ Figure B _____

6. Find the volume for each figure.

   Figure A _____ Figure B _____

Module 8: Section B Lesson 3

Name _____

Complete the following chart for
Figures 1, 2 and 3. (Assume cm cubes.)

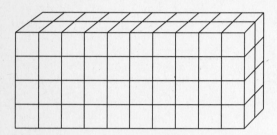

Figure 1

Figure 2

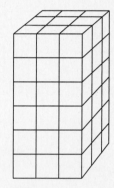

Figure 3

	Area of Base	Number of Layers	Volume
Figure 1:	1.	2.	3.
Figure 2:	4.	5.	6.
Figure 3:	7.	8.	9.

Module 8: Section B Lesson 3

Name _____

Fill in the chart for the figures below.
(Assume cm cubes.)

Figure 2

Figure 1

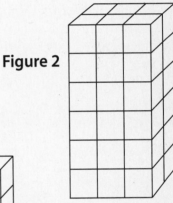

Figure 3

	Area of Base	Number of Layers	Volume
Figure 1:	1.	2.	3.
Figure 2:	4.	5.	6.
Figure 3:	7.	8.	9.

Name _____

Estimate the volume in cubic centimeters for rectangular prisms with these dimensions. If the estimate is greater than 1,000 cm³, find the exact volume.

1. 10 cm by 12 cm by 18 cm _____

2. 13 cm by 14 cm by 14 cm _____

3. 8 cm by 19 cm by 21 cm _____

4. 28 cm by 7 cm by 11 cm _____

5. 5 cm by 5 cm by 6 cm _____

6. 17 cm by 8 cm by 14 cm _____

Module 8: Section B Lesson 3

Name _____

Answer the following questions.

1. A thousands' cube holds exactly
   how many liters of water? _____

2. What are the dimensions
   of a thousands' cube? _____

3. One cubic decimeter equals
   how many liters of water? _____

4. How many cubic centimeters
   are contained in a ones' cube? _____

5. How many ones' cubes are
   contained in a thousands' cube? _____

6. In the metric system, what does
   the expression milli- mean? _____

7. What fraction of a liter is a milliliter?

_____

Module 8: Section B Lesson 4

Name _____

A rectangular prism contains 1 liter
of water.

1. How many cubic centimeters
are in this prism? _____

2. What is the volume of
Figure A in liters? _____

3. What is the volume of
Figure A in milliliters? _____

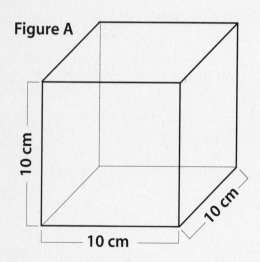

Figure A

10 cm

10 cm

10 cm

Module 8: Section B Lesson 4

Name _____

In two ways, state the area of the base and the height of three triangular prisms that have the given volume.

120 cubic units

1. area of base _____   **2.** height _____

3. area of base _____   **4.** height _____

36 cubic units

5. area of base _____   **6.** height _____

7. area of base _____   **8.** height _____

60 cubic units

9. area of base _____   **10.** height _____

11. area of base _____   **12.** height _____

Name _____

If a triangular prism has a height of 10 layers, and its base looks like the following diagram on a grid, what do you estimate its volume to be?

1.

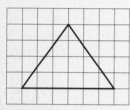

_____

2.

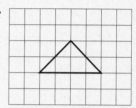

_____

If a cylinder has a height of 5 layers, and its base looks like the following on a diagram, what do you estimate its volume to be?

3.

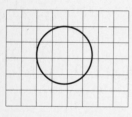

_____

4.

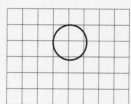

_____

Module 8: Section B Lesson 4

Name _____

Materials: grid paper

Here are some common objects with actual dimensions. Make a scale drawing of each object on a sheet of grid paper. Write the scale you used.

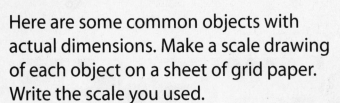

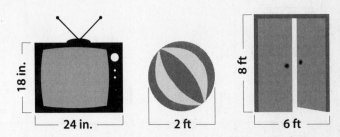

Height	1. _____	2. _____	3. _____
Width	4. _____	5. _____	6. _____

Module 8: Section C Lesson 5

Name _____

Find the scale used for each object in the chart.

Object	Actual Dimensions	Drawing Dimensions	Scale
Book	8 in. × 4 in.	8 in. × 4 in.	
SOUP	4 in. × 3 in.	8 in. × 6 in.	
	4 ft × 3 ft	12 in. × 9 in.	

Module 8: Section C Lesson 5

Name _____

Make flowcharts for the following
activities:

1. making scrambled eggs

2. taking a book out of the library

Module 8: Section C Lesson 6

Name _____

Here is a flowchart that shows the steps involved in getting ready for school. Circle the steps that you think are out of order. Add any steps that you think are missing.

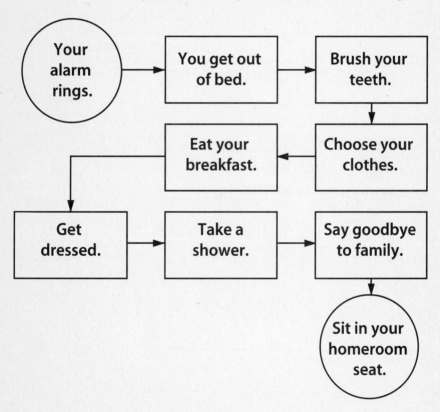

Your alarm rings. → You get out of bed. → Brush your teeth.

Brush your teeth. ↓ Choose your clothes.

Eat your breakfast. ← Choose your clothes.

Get dressed. → Take a shower. → Say goodbye to family.

Say goodbye to family. ↓ Sit in your homeroom seat.

Module 8: Section C Lesson 6

Name _____

There is a sugarless bubblegum machine outside the supermarket. Every nickel you put in gives you back 2 balls of bubblegum. Write the function rule for this machine and show at least 5 inputs and 5 outputs.

1. Function Rule _____

2. Input   **a.** _____   **3.** Output   **a.** _____

                b. _____   **b.** _____

                c. _____   **c.** _____

                d. _____   **d.** _____

                e. _____   **e.** _____

Skill Worksheet 245

Module 8: Section C Lesson 7

Name _____

Find the missing numbers for the
following Input/Output tables.

1.

Input	1	2	3	?	5
Output	3	6	9	12	15

_____

2.

Input	2	4	6	8	10
Output	1	?	3	4	5

_____

3.

Input	2	4	5	8	11
Output	0	0	0	?	0

_____

4.

Input	10	?	30	40	50
Output	5	10	15	20	25

_____

Module 8: Section C Lesson 7

Name _____

Match the following function rule with the correct Input/Output table.

1. $n \times 3$

a.

Inputs	1	2	3	4	5
Output	3	8	13	18	23

_____

2. $(n \times 5) - 2$

b.

Inputs	5	10	15	20	25
Output	8	13	18	23	28

_____

3. $n + 3$

c.

Inputs	4	8	12	16	20
Output	2	4	6	8	10

_____

4. $\frac{n}{2}$

d.

Inputs	5	10	15	20	25
Output	15	30	45	60	75

_____

Name _____

Match the following function rule with the correct Input/Output table.

1. $n + 7$

_____

a.

Inputs	25	30	35	40	45
Output	5	6	7	8	9

2. $\left(\frac{n}{2}\right) + 1$

_____

b.

Inputs	1	2	3	4	5
Output	8	9	10	11	12

3. $\frac{n}{5}$

_____

c.

Inputs	2	4	6	8	10
Output	2	3	4	5	6

4. $n \times 4$

_____

d.

Inputs	10	20	30	40	50
Output	40	80	120	160	200

Module 8: Section C Lesson 7

Name _____

Look at the following scale drawing of a clock. The ratio is 1 ft: 1in.

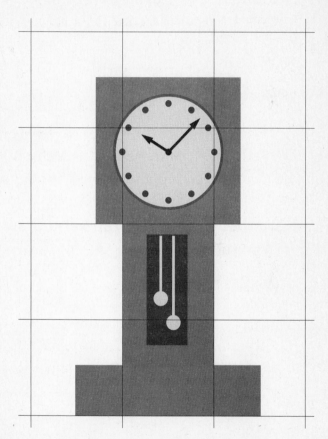

1. What is the actual size of the clock? _____

Module 8: Section D Lesson 8

Name _____

Use ratios to help you answer Exercises 1-2.

1. Use the ratio 1 ft : $\frac{1}{2}$ in. to draw a
   scale model of a painting that is 24 ft by 36 ft.

2. Choose another appropriate ratio and draw
   another scale model.

Module 8: Section D Lesson 8

Name _____

Here is a scale drawing with a ratio of 1 ft: $\frac{1}{2}$ in. What are the dimensions of the actual tree?

_____

Module 8: Section D Lesson 8

Name _____

Draw two scale models of a window
that is 4 ft by 3 ft using the ratios below.

SKILL
252
WORKSHEET

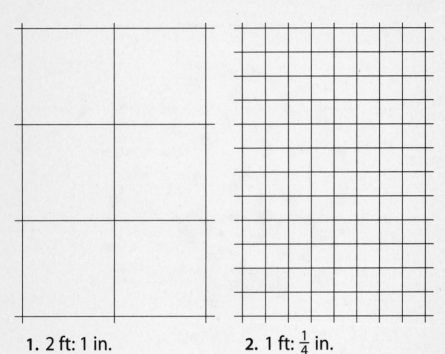

1. 2 ft: 1 in.

2. 1 ft: $\frac{1}{4}$ in.

Module 8: Section D Lesson 8

Name _____

Predict the missing output. Write the correct function rule for each chart.

Input	1	2	3	4	5
Output	2	4	6	8	?

1. Missing output _____

2. Function Rule _____

Input	4	11	13	21	24
Output	8	15	17	25	?

3. Missing output _____

4. Function Rule _____

Module 8: Section D Lesson 9

Name _____

Predict the missing outputs. Write the correct function rule for each chart.

SKILL
254
WORKSHEET

Input	1	3	5	7	9	11	13
Output	5	15	25	35	45	?	?

1. Missing outputs _____

2. Function Rule _____

Input	2	4	6	8	10	12	14
Output	14	28	42	56	70	?	?

3. Missing outputs _____

4. Function Rule _____

Module 8: Section D Lesson 9

Name _____

Use the chart to answer Exercises 1-4.

1. Predict the number of cubes released at 8 min.

_____

2. Describe the function rule for this machine.

_____

Time (in minutes)	Cubes released
1	6
2	11
3	16
4	21
5	26

3. How long would it take to fill a box that holds 76 cubes? _____

4. Graph the data in at least one way.

Module 8: Section D Lesson 9

Name _____

Use the chart to answer Exercises 1-4.

1. Predict the number of cubes released at 10 min.

_____

2. Describe the function rule for this machine.

_____

3. How long would it take to fill a box that holds 75 cubes? _____

4. Graph the data in at least one way.

Time (in minutes)	Cubes released
1	7
2	11
3	15
4	19
5	23

Module 8: Section D Lesson 9

Notes

Notes